THE BRITISH ACADEMY

Jewish and Christian Apocalypses

By

F. Crawford Burkitt, M.A., D.D.

Norrisian Professor of Divinity in the
University of Cambridge
Fellow of the British Academy

The Schweich Lectures

1913

Wipf & Stock
PUBLISHERS
Eugene, Oregon

Wipf and Stock Publishers
199 W 8th Ave, Suite 3
Eugene, OR 97401

Jewish and Christian Apocalypses
By F. Crawford Burkitt
ISBN 13: 978-1-55635-062-7
ISBN 10: 1-55635-062-7
Publication date 12/4/2006
Previously published by Oxford University Press, 1914

TO THE MEMORY OF

SAMUEL ROLLES DRIVER

THE FIRST OF THE SCHWEICH LECTURERS

כל העוסק בתורה לשמה... נהנין
ממנו עצה ותושיה בינה וגבורה

Aboth vi 1

PREFACE

THIS book contains the three Schweich Lectures for 1913, printed almost exactly as they were delivered last November. The only change of importance is that I have divided the third Lecture into its two constituent parts, so as to keep the specifically Christian variety of Apocalypse in a class by itself.

In the Lectures I attempted to confine myself as much as possible to what I believe to be the fundamental idea which underlies the great series of Jewish Apocalypses, *viz.* the idea of the imminent Judgement to Come, and further, to exhibit this Idea in connexion with what I believe to be both its true historical setting and the ultimate cause of its manifestation. That which gives the Apocalypses vitality is the great struggle between Religion and Civilization, of which the Maccabean Martyrs are the symbol. I omit the adjectives. My readers themselves, according as they view the thing, can say 'between spiritual Religion and material Civilization' or 'between fanatical Religion and enlightened Civilization,'—and they will judge the Apocalypses accordingly. But it seemed to me worth while to exhibit the Apocalypses as clearly as possible from this quite definite and particular point of view, and therefore I found it inadvisable to expand what I had said by introducing other points of view or more details into the printed form of the Lectures.

What I have added will be found in the separate Appendices. These will, I hope, explain themselves to the specialists for whom they were primarily written. They will at least serve to shew that I have not ventured to make sweeping generalisations about this department of ancient literature without making a somewhat minute study of the principal documents.

The year 1913 saw a grand edition of all the Old Testament 'Apocrypha' and 'Pseudepigrapha' brought out under the able and stimulating editorship of Dr, now Canon, R. H. Charles. Students of the Book of Enoch are under a deep debt of gratitude to Dr Charles, who now has edited it three times in English and once in Ethiopic. Is it not time that a literal English translation should be accessible to all? Poor students of theology can be expected to have read Daniel, for it is in the Bible; they can be expected to have read Second Esdras, for it is at least in 'the Apocrypha'. But the cheapest way of getting at the plain text of Enoch is still to try and pick up a second-hand copy of one of the reprints of Laurence's translation, and this generally comes to about three-and-sixpence. This translation was pioneer work. It was most creditable as a first attempt, but like all such efforts, especially when made on a bad text, it is generally inadequate, often obscure, and to young students often positively misleading. On any theory of the Book of Enoch either of Dr Charles's translations is vastly superior. I am not thinking of the needs of teachers and professors, but of young students and ordinary clergymen. Is it impossible to hope that Dr Charles and the Clarendon Press will prepare a plain translation for us? If not, I hope that some one else who knows Ethiopic will make one. If he does so, let me further beg him to make as few emendations as possible,—he should follow Dr Charles's MS *g* almost always,—and when he feels bound to make an emendation let it be always quite clear to the reader what the transmitted text is. A text so prepared would be useful to teachers and could be bought by students, for I do not think it need cost more than a shilling.

F. C. BURKITT

Westroad Corner, Cambridge
March, 1914

CONTENTS

PAGE

I. THE APOCALYPTIC IDEA 1

II. THE BOOK OF ENOCH 17

III. THE MINOR JEWISH APOCALYPSES 34

IV. EARLY CHRISTIAN APOCALYPTIC WRITING 44

APPENDIX I: ON THE GREEK TEXT OF ENOCH

1. *The Descent of the Angels* 53
2. *The Prologue to Enoch* 55
3. *Enoch and the Valleys of the Dead* 65
4. *Miscellaneous Conjectures* 68
5. *On the Astronomical teaching of Enoch* 70

APPENDIX II: ON THE MARTYRDOM OF ISAIAH 72

APPENDIX III: ON SOME OTHER KINDS OF APOCALYPSES . 75

INDEX 79

ILLUSTRATION

THE GIZEH MS. OF ENOCH, p. 23 . . . . . *To face p.* 1

THE GIZEH MS. OF ENOCH, p. 23.

The Book of Enoch begins in the middle of line 8 (marked with a cross).

JEWISH AND CHRISTIAN APOCALYPSES.

I. THE APOCALYPTIC IDEA.

THE subject announced for the present series of Schweich Lectures is "Jewish and Christian Apocalypses". It is a subject upon which much has been written of late years, especially by specialists for specialists. Besides this frankly specialist literature there has not been wanting a great measure of recognition of the importance, in a general way, of these Apocalypses and the state of mind which they reflect, for the history of Early Christianity. But the Apocalypses themselves are still unfamiliar to most people, and indeed there are a good many reasons against their becoming popular in the present day. Both as wholes and in detail they are strange and foreign to our ways of thinking and writing: they need, in fact, a great deal of what is called 'Introduction' to make them comprehensible at all. Before coming, therefore, to the Apocalypses or to the circumstances that called them forth, I wish to make a few remarks on certain ideas and conceptions with which the Apocalypses are fundamentally concerned.

The Sistine Chapel is familiar to all in this travelled age. As you all know, it is the private chapel of the Popes and it was decorated by the greatest artists of the time. The Popes for whom the work was done, and the artists who did it, were all profoundly influenced by the Renaissance, by the revival of the literature, the art, the ideas of heathen Greece and Rome. Those who do not admire the Sistine Chapel as an example of Christian Art generally complain that it seems to them pagan: at least it is free from the reproach of being overmuch mediaeval. Let us consider for a moment what the scheme of decoration really is. We will not go into the Chapel as if it were a mere picture-gallery, walking about freely from point to point. We will take no looking-glasses in our hands or lie on our backs to examine the ceiling. No doubt persons attending Mass have in all ages turned their heads occasionally from side to side and looked up at the roof. Those who do so at the Sistine Chapel see on their left scenes from the Old Testament and on their right the fulfilment in the

New. If they glance at the roof, they see the creation of the world and the beginnings of history as taught in Scripture and tradition. The pious worshipper will perhaps not care thus to look about him. But there is one thing which he cannot well help seeing. He cannot raise his eyes to adore the consecrated Host without being confronted with the Last Judgement. Behind the Priest, behind the Altar, behind the lighted candles, behind the sacred drama of worship, the Last Judgement is always there. The only thing that stands between the Christian worshipper and Hell is the Priest and the Altar.

The symbolism of the Last Judgement, as presented in Christian Churches, is not always exactly the same as in the Sistine Chapel. At Ulm, and formerly in many English Churches, it was represented on the Chancel Arch, so that the Altar was exhibited as the one open door through which the worshipper might take refuge. But however it might be figured, it stood in the centre of conviction, both in popular belief and in the official creed. The Pope's Chapel, for all the classical detail in the paintings, faithfully reflects the Christian scheme of things: behind everything the Last Judgement looms in the background, universal, inevitable.

The guide-books tell us that Michaelangelo's great picture owes a great deal to Dante. I have no doubt that this is true in the sense in which the statement is made, i. e. in the arrangement of details. Nevertheless there is a sense in which Dante's poem marks the triumph of a quite different order of ideas, which robs the idea of the Last Judgement of most of its significance. Dante goes to the Other World, he sees the dead in Paradise, in Purgatory, or in Hell. For all intents and purposes the Last Judgement has no meaning for them: they are judged already. After such and such a time or mode of probation one by one the souls in Purgatory will leave it to join the souls in Paradise, just as one by one they had arrived. The Other World is a *place*, which individuals enter one by one when they die; the conception of the Last Judgement, on the other hand, makes the Other World a *time*, an era, which all individuals experience simultaneously, a "Divine Event to which all Nature moves". It is this Divine Event that is set forth by the Apocalypses. The doctrine of the Apocalypses is the doctrine of the Last Judgement.

For the study of Early Christianity it is most important to keep in mind the distinction between the doctrine of a Last Judgement and other forms of belief in retributive justice and in life beyond the grave. This is particularly the case when it comes to a question of origins. That the Powers above us are just and that evil will not go in the end unpunished has been the conviction of many races of mankind: it is not necessary to look for a historical nexus every time this belief finds expression. The same may be said of belief in the persistence of a man's spirit or ghost. And it is an easy, though not a logically necessary step, to combine the two beliefs and to hold that the comparative happiness or misery of a man in his future life depends on his past. Systems so different as Indian and Egyptian Religion agree in this. But the notion of a future general Assize, at which all wrong will be put right, not always with special reference to individual cases, is a peculiar conception. It is certainly not universal, or even widespread, and we may therefore suppose that it required a very special train of circumstances to develop it.

One thing appears to me to be quite certain. It seems to me certain that the doctrine of a future general Assize held no place in the Graeco-Roman world, apart from the beliefs of Jews and Christians. The period between the eras of Alexander the Great and the Emperor Constantine, those six centuries during which Christianity grew up, was an age of syncretism, of the mingling of religions, a period during which European civilization was especially influenced by Oriental beliefs. It was the age of the Mystery-religions, the religions of Isis, of Mithra, of Attis. The dominant philosophies, as we are more and more coming to see, were the result of the blending of Greek thought with Oriental beliefs and teachings. Oriental Astrology was in itself a religious philosophy; it was an attempt to formulate the influences which to a certain degree moulded the lives of all the dwellers under the roof of heaven. One school of Philosophers, the Stoics, even taught the doctrine of a future general conflagration, but this is quite a different thing from the Last Judgement. The Stoic conflagration merely started everything over again, to retread the old circle. Graeco-Roman religion, speaking generally, did not see in History the working-out of a Divine Purpose.

I said just now that the doctrine of a Last Judgement required a very special set of circumstances for its development. It will not be a part of my aim in these Lectures to trace the growth of this doctrine among the Jews from its origins. It is commonly said to have been taken over by the Jews from Zoroastrianism, and there may be some truth in this view. But for us the more important thing is to notice that the seed fell on congenial soil, from wherever it may have originally come. What I wish specially to emphasize is the difference between Judaism and the contemporary Hellenistic, Graeco-Roman, beliefs. Let us grant for the moment that the

Jewish hope was coloured by Zoroastrianism : Mithraism, in any case, was in great part ultimately derived from Persia. Why, then, was a doctrine of Last Judgement so prominent in the one religion and not in the other ?

Here we come, in a very real sense, to the heart of our subject. I believe the main peculiarities, the main *differentia*, of post-Alexandrian Judaism to arise directly from the actual history of the Jews, in a word, to be the result of the great struggle between Judaism and Hellenism.

It is during the two centuries and a half that extend from the Maccabean Rising to the Destruction of Jerusalem by Titus, from 170 B. C. to 70 A. D., that the world in general is confronted with the Jewish Nation. Before the Captivity its history had been simply that of one among many petty nationalities of Palestine. The annals of Sargon or of Sennacherib betray no consciousness that the subjects of the King of Jerusalem were different in thought or customs from other people. After the Return the Jews had lived unnoticed in quiet. After the Destruction of Jerusalem, again, the direct political power of Judaism is gone; the Jews become a Church, an international Society, rather than a Nation in the ordinary sense of the word. But in the interval Judaism had played a truly national part; it became during those two-and-a-half centuries a kingdom of this world, an alternative to Civilization as then understood, actually before the eyes of men.

It is a curious fact that the parts of Israelite history with which most of us are familiar are concerned with the preparation of the Jews for their peculiar rôle rather than with the part they actually played in general history. The kingdom over which the princes of the House of David ruled made very little mark on the ancient world, and when the hill-fortress of Jerusalem stood in the way of the great empire of Babylonia it fell, and the kingdom of Judah fell with it. The Jewish State collapsed, and there was nothing to indicate to an outsider that any part of the social organisation would survive. As a matter of fact, as we all know, the religion of the Jews—or at least of a part of them—had undergone a strange and unique development, the result of which was that it did not die with its mother the old Jewish State. Two generations later, when there is a change of Empires, some of the heads of the Jewish communities in Babylon are still Jews, and they return to set the life in their old home going once more, and to worship the God of their fathers as aforetime.

The history of the age of Ezra is full of unsolved historical problems, but certain things are clear enough. It was no doubt a day of small things. The returned exiles aspired to play no great political part; their chief desire was to be left alone to practise their religion. But insignificant as they might be in numbers and immediate influence, they were now a peculiar people. They were quite conscious of the fact themselves, and made their neighbours conscious of it. They were the People: the rest of the world were Gentiles. They now possessed the Law of God in black and white, a Law that had been given to them to keep at all costs.

From the days of Ezra begins that most characteristic product of Judaism—the Study of the Law. The community existed for the sake of the Temple and its worship, for the sake of the ritual practised at the Temple. To surround Jerusalem with a wall, and gradually to raise up a fence for the Tora, as a later age phrased it—that was a sufficient ambition. The Word of God had been already given to them, and so the race of the Prophets came to an end and that of the Scribes took its place.

The work of the Scribes was far more important than it was once thought to have been. The wise men of Israel who came after Ezra had the Law already, but it was they who brought the Prophets into the form in which we read them, and the Psalms, whatever ancient fragments they may possibly contain, were in the main their work. To the Prophets it had been given to make the Religion of Israel, but the Scribes made the Bible. It is difficult, when we think of the immense effect that the Old Testament has had, to find words high enough to describe the importance of the work of the Scribes for after generations. And yet it was secondary and derivative. The Scribes had not in themselves the direct and masterful authority that belonged to the Prophets who went before them. They were not commissioned themselves to say 'Thus saith the LORD'. And so when the crisis came we find a new phenomenon. The Jew who feels himself to have a new message for his brethren shelters himself under a pseudonym. The original literature of the two centuries and a half that preceded the capture of Jerusalem is either anonymous, or it professes to be the work of some worthy of old time. It is a remarkable fact, that during the period when the Jewish Nation was actually playing a great part in the world's history, a part which was the direct outcome of the ideas which animated the people, there are hardly any avowed Jewish writers, till we come to the commentator Philo and to the Christians. It was a literary age, and in it a great quantity of Jewish literature was produced, some of which had great influence. But almost all of it was published in the name of some ancient hero, as a vision of the future which he had received.

It is well, I think, to remind ourselves at the outset that the authorship of the Book of Daniel is no isolated problem. Baruch, Ezra, Solomon, Moses, the Twelve Patriarchs, Noah, Enoch, Adam, —all these had Apocalypses or Testaments fathered upon them. It is difficult to know in particular cases how far the pseudonymity was an understood literary artifice and how far it was really deceptive. What, I think, is clear is that both authors and readers believed that if any Revelation from God was true, it could not be new. It must have been given to the great Saints of antiquity. The Christian Apocalypse of John, as we read it, may be a compilation of different dates, or a reissue of an earlier book, but in this respect the core of it breathes a new spirit. "*I John*, your brother and companion in tribulation, . . . *I* heard a voice which said, Write to Ephesus and the rest of the Churches":—this is new. It is a new message, given to the contemporary Seer, and it marks the end of the type of writing which we are to study.

The great spiritual crisis that befel the Jews of the second century before our era was not the result of any development of Jewish thought. It was brought on from without. To the pious Jew was offered by Antiochus Epiphanes the alternative of death or assimilation to the Heathen world around him, and he chose rather to die. And here, as in so many other crises of history the saying was verified that whoso hateth his present life shall keep it and obtain life in a greater and larger sense. It was under Antiochus that Israel rose up once more to be a nation, baptized to a new life in the blood of the Martyrs.

I am not going to attempt to tell the story of the great struggle between Judaism and Hellenism, or to appraise the great debt that even our modern world owes to the Jews for preserving elements of religion that were absent from the rather vulgar Hellenic ideals of the Seleucid Empire. The point I wish to make is this, that during the period we are considering Judaism came to play an imperial part in the history of civilization, and that as a consequence Judaism learned—the modern catchword is convenient—'learned to think imperially'.

What I mean may be illustrated by a comparison between the prophecies against the nations in Ezekiel and Jeremiah as contrasted with those in the Book of Daniel. In Jeremiah and Ezekiel we have announcements of Divine vengeance upon the enemies of Israel, but it is all piecemeal and detached.[1] In Daniel, on the other hand, there is a philosophy of universal History: "the great Gentile kingdoms, like the Greek supremacy of the Seleucids and Ptolemies which seemed so overwhelming and terrible, are shewn as phases in a world process whose end is the Kingdom of God".[2] Even now 'the Most High ruleth in the kingdom of men, and giveth it to whomsoever He will' (Dan iv 17). Intensely patriotic as was the author of the book of Daniel, there is something cosmopolitan about his outlook on the world. The Stone cut out without hands does not merely claim the right to exist: it is the conscious rival of the Imperial Statue. In other words, Judaism is to the author of Daniel a cosmic world-religion, and that not merely by detached and occasional glimpses, but consciously and all the time.

Meanwhile the persecuted Saints of the Most High, the Jews who are faithful to the true religion, are in the utmost extremity of distress. Surely God (they thought) will soon, very soon, arise to avenge His own and bring in His Kingdom that will last for ever. Here you have the other side of the picture of Jewish world-religion, the other side of the struggle of ideas between Jewish Religion and Greek Civilization, and this is the expectation of the Kingdom of God and the belief that its Coming is imminent. The Kingdom of God—that is the central idea. It is the New Age, the new state of things that will come about when the great agony has ended by God's victorious intervention on behalf of His Saints, when He comes, or sends His Representative to come, to set the world right.

In the two following Lectures I intend to describe some of the outstanding features of certain of the Apocalypses in which this hope found its most characteristic expression, and to discuss certain problems connected with their interpretation. But before coming to details I wish to say something about the influences which ultimately threw almost all these Apocalypses out of favour. I feel it is most important that we should see from the beginning what they signify as a class, what their function was in Jewish thought generally. If we get them into focus as a whole, we shall avoid regarding with disproportioned attention individual features and individual difficulties which are, after all, of subordinate importance.

It would perhaps be unphilosophical to assert that the expectation of the Kingdom of God, of God's approaching intervention, was caused

[1] See especially Ezek xxix 15; the Prophet is unable to imagine a new arrangement of the world he had known, a world with no Egypt at all.

[2] Edwyn Bevan, *Jerusalem under the High Priests*, p. 86.

by the great struggle between Judaism and Hellenism, between the Jewish and Gentile ideals. But this expectation was certainly stimulated and coloured by the struggle. While the struggle lasted Israel was playing a great part on the world's stage, great, that is, from the point of view of the play of ideas and of their subsequent influence, and Israelite thought re-echoed the national activity. After a while came the reaction, or rather I should say, after a while there came a wholly new set of national conditions, and Jewish thought underwent a reconstruction to suit these altered conditions. In the year 70 A. D., after the capture of Jerusalem, the Jewish State was destroyed. Great departments of the national life ceased altogether to exist materially; if they continued at all, they could only continue as ideas, in (so to speak) a spiritual form. The Jewish State, the sacrificial worship, the office of the priests, the Feasts, the pilgrimages to the Feasts, all that in the New Testament is associated with the Sadducees or the Herodians—all these disappeared. To quote the words of the Apocalypse of Baruch, 'Zion hath been taken from us, and we have nothing now save the Mighty One and His Law' (lxxxv 3).

It was a wonderful achievement for Jewish Religion to have rallied at all after the sack of Jerusalem in the year 70, and again after Bar Cochba's rebellion two generations later in Hadrian's time. It is not surprising that such catastrophes should have modified Jewish Religion: the wonder is that it should have survived at all, and that it should have survived in such a way as to retain real continuity with the past. When it is stated that Rabbinic Pharisaism after the destruction of the Temple differs largely from Pharisaism before that date we ought, I venture to think, be very careful that we express this obvious truth in such a way as to be just to Johanan ben Zakkai and the other founders of the Rabbinical Religion.[1] Some of you

[1] The name of Johanan ben Zakkai is hardly known among Christians, but to him more than any man is due the survival of Judaism as an organized religious system after the Destruction of Jerusalem in 70 and the cessation of the Sacrifices. He had been a pupil of Hillel, so that he was probably only a few years junior to S. Paul. During the Siege, Johanan b. Zakkai escaped out of Jerusalem and obtained permission from Titus to retire to the village of Jabne or Jamnia, and teach there openly. When the news of the fall of Jerusalem came to Jamnia, Johanan's disciple Joshua b. Ḥanania cried out 'Woe to us, because the place is destroyed where they make propitiation for the sins of Israel!' But Johanan answered 'My son, let it not grieve thee; we have yet one propitiation equal to it, and what is that but the bestowal of kindnesses?—even as it is written "I desired kindness and not sacrifice".' Compare Matt xii 7 and the saying of Simon the Just in *Aboth* i 2.

A good account of Johanan is to be found in Bacher's *Agada der Tannaiten*, ed. 2, pp. 22–42. In N.T. style Johanan's name would be John the son of Zacchaeus.

know, some of you perhaps know by heart, the first two chapters of *Aboth*, where the chain of Teachers is set out from the men of the Great Synagogue who learned from Ezra, through Hillel and Shammai, to Johanan ben Zakkai. The succession is genuine. It would ill become me as an Anglican Churchman, who values the idea of apostolical succession and the organic continuity implied by it, to regard the spiritual descent of Johanan from Ezra otherwise than with respect and sympathy. The religion of Johanan ben Zakkai is a legitimate child of the religion of Ezra. I am only putting before you the view that it is not the only legitimate child; and further, that in adapting itself to the altered conditions of existence after 70 the Rabbinical Religion was obliged to abandon part of the inheritance of former generations.

One of the first problems before the newly-organized Judaism was to make a fence for the Law in a very direct sense, to fix in fact the limits of the Canon of Scripture. By 70 A. D., indeed, the main contents were beyond controversy, but the final delimitation had yet to be made. Among the Jews, as among the Christians, the growth of the Canon of Scripture had been an almost imperceptible and natural process, extending over a series of generations. No one can say precisely when the Books of Kings among the Jews, or the Acts of the Apostles among the Christians became Canonical Scripture. The final stage we can just trace to some extent, because it is more or less a conscious process. The wall is already there, and the last comer is helped over it, not without protests, just as the coping stone is put on. Every one has heard of the saying of Rabbi Akiba about the *inclusion* of the Song of Songs—'all the Hagiographa are holy, but the Song of Songs is Holy of Holies'—but about the *rejection* of the Writings that in the end were rejected we know very little. "It is for us", says Wellhausen, "hard to understand why Koheleth was accepted and Ben Sira not, why Baruch was excluded and Daniel not, why Esther was appreciated and 1 Maccabees not."[1] A more or less satisfactory explanation can indeed be given in each case, the result being known, but one feels that almost equally satisfactory explanations would have been forthcoming, had the result been different.

However that may be, the Canon of Scripture was defined, with the inevitable result that the rejected books gradually became forgotten and ceased to exercise any influence on Jewish thought. And indeed, whatever surprise we may feel about the disappearance of particular books, it is easy to see that most of the Apocalypses would have been out of place in the reformed Judaism of Jamnia and Tiberias. But

[1] Bleek's *Einleitung* (1878), p. 552.

that is no reason for underestimating their part in the older religious life of Jerusalem and the dominions of Herod Antipas, in the days when the Temple was yet standing and the Jewish State was still a reality. Above all, these documents are important to the Christian student, because he is less concerned with the reconstruction of Judaism under Johanan ben Zakkai and his successors, than with the general conditions of Judaism before the Destruction of Jerusalem.

Most important of all is the case of the Book of Enoch. There is a curious passage about this famous work in Tertullian, who happens to quote the Book of Enoch for the sake of the tradition that the fallen Angel Azael taught women the use of cosmetics and jewellery. Tertullian, having remarked that he knows the scripture of Enoch is not received by some on the ground that it is not admitted into the Jewish Collection, goes on to say: 'since Enoch in the same Scripture also predicted concerning the Lord, by us Christians the view is not at all to be rejected that it does concern us, and we read that all scripture which is suitable for edification is divinely inspired (2 Tim iii 16). That by the Jews it should seem to have been afterwards rejected, like most of the other things that have a Christian ring, is not so very wonderful, i. e. if they have not received certain Scriptures about Him whom they would not receive when He was speaking to them in person.'[1] And Tertullian adds that the Book of Enoch has also in its favour the apostolic testimony of the Epistle of Jude.

The fierce and dogmatic Christian rhetorician, himself more than half a heretic, does not express himself in the language of modern criticism, but I venture to think his words have a real meaning for the historian of ideas. What were the reasons that made 'Enoch' an honoured book to Tertullian and his Church, that caused it to be quoted in Jude and Barnabas, and referred to besides in 1 Peter and elsewhere in the New Testament, and (what is more important) made it part of the background of the earliest Christian teaching, of the teaching of Jesus Himself? What were the reasons that caused it to be proscribed and forgotten by orthodox Judaism, so that hardly a memory of it survives in Rabbinical literature?

We cannot answer these questions with the cheery assurance of the apologists of a past generation, and say that Enoch was rejected because it was a forgery, while Canonical Scripture is genuine and historical. We live in an age which has fully realised that neither Esther nor Daniel is historical, an age which does not take its beliefs about the origin of man and the universe from Genesis any more than it does from Enoch. We have rather to consider, as well as we can,

[1] *De Cultu Fem.* i 3.

what the Book of Enoch must have meant to the Jew of the times of Alexander Jannaeus and of Herod, to the Jew and the Christian of the time of the Destruction of Jerusalem, to the Christian of later ages.

Modern scholars are pretty well agreed as to the Palestinian origin of the Book of Enoch, and that it had attained its present form before the Christian Era. What is in dispute is the original form of its constituent parts and the dates to which they should be assigned. For our purpose just now this does not matter so much. It is not disputed that the book quoted in the Epistle of Jude is our Enoch; it is our Enoch, the work preserved in full in Ethiopic and for the first third in Greek, that the early Christians read and the Rabbis rejected. And the problem before us is to discover why this Palestinian book attracted the one party and failed to attract the other.

We must find a general reason, for none of the Apocalyptic writings, with the exception of Daniel, was received by the reformed Judaism of Jamnia and Tiberias. The only reason for the exception must have been that the position of the Book of Daniel in the Jewish Canon of Scripture was already assured before the Destruction of Jerusalem. This view, it may be remarked in passing, is borne out by the particular respect shewn to it by such widely separated representatives of 1st century Jewish thought as the Synoptic Gospels and Josephus. But Daniel is a solitary exception. Every one of the others, the Apocalypses or Testaments of Adam, Enoch, Noah, Abraham, the Twelve Patriarchs, the Book of Jubilees, the Assumption of Moses, the Apocalypses of Ezra and of Baruch, were all excluded. Indeed their claims do not seem to have been seriously considered. Among the Christians, on the other hand, they were long current, and Christian Apocalypses, such as the Ascension of Isaiah, were composed in imitation of them, not to speak of more original works, such as the Apocalypse of Peter and the canonical Apocalypse of John. After a time the Apocalypses fell out of favour in the Christian Church also, as the expectation of the speedy end of all things gradually faded away. But they had been rejected from the first by the Jewish Schools that survived the Destruction of Jerusalem.

Naturally the word 'rejection' does not mean that Johanan ben Zakkai and his scholars tried the claims of Enoch and, on consideration, came to a view unfavourable to its canonicity. Before a book becomes canonical, it must become at least interesting, and we have to find out why the book that was so interesting to Jude and the Christians was not interesting to Johanan and those who worked with him. Official canonicity is only the final seal: the fate of a book has generally been determined long before the official decision is pronounced.

I have quoted to you a piece from Tertullian about Enoch, to exhibit to you the motives that made it an honoured book in the Church. What saying shall we take to sum up the reasons why the Apocalypses were not preserved by the Synagogue? I will venture to take as my text the saying of Johanan ben Zakkai, that God revealed to Abram this world, but the world to come He did not reveal to him.[1] I believe that this saying really implies the renunciation of the Apocalyptic idea, the notion that the Kingdom of God was an external state of things which was just upon the point of being manifested, and (as a corollary) that the person of insight could know something about it beforehand. It was this idea that inspires the whole series of Jewish Apocalypses, that was the central thought of the earliest preaching of Christianity, that intoxicated the Jewish people in their wild struggle with Rome. Johanan ben Zakkai, as you all know, had no false hopes about that struggle. He kept a sober mind, like Jeremiah before him. He saw the inevitable destruction of Jerusalem; and so, when the crash came, and the sacrifices came to an end, he was prepared to guide Jewish thought and religion into new channels, not less profound, if necessarily more narrow, than those along which they ran of old. He was content to let the future age wait for God's good time, when it should please Him to reveal it, and perhaps it was as well that he could not foresee the future, or he might not have had the courage to begin his epoch-making work in the Vineyard at Jamnia.

We read in the Gospel that Wisdom is justified of her children. Like certain of the sayings in *Pirḳe Aboth* the exact meaning of this pronouncement in its original context is somewhat obscure, and the wise have held differing opinions about it. But if we may for once take it in the sense that the wisdom of a course of action is to be inferred from its results, then we may recognise the wisdom both of the early Christians and of those Jews who rallied round Johanan ben Zakkai. The work of these two companies was very different, their aims, their ideals were different, and it is therefore not surprising that they travelled along different roads. 'The Kingdom of God at hand'—that was the Christian watchword. A New World, a wholly new

[1] *Ber. rab.* 44 (on Gen xv 18): העולם הזה גלה לו׳ אבל העולם הבא לא גלה לו. R. Aḳiba, on the contrary, said that God revealed to Abram both this world and that which is to come—but Aḳiba, unlike Johanan ben Zakkai, believed that the Kingdom of God was at hand, and lost his life as an adherent of Bar Cochba.

state of things is on the point of arriving: watch and be ready, and above all do not cumber yourselves with your old possessions, your old traditions, your old affections. I am not asking you to forget the personal influence of Jesus upon those who accepted Him as their Master, for indeed without it you lose the cord that both binds the Christians together and supplies the current of their enthusiasm. But that enthusiasm of the early Christians was directed to the Good Time Coming. And the historian of religion can now see quite clearly what advantages this detachment gave to the Christians. From our vantage-ground we can see very well that the Jewish State had become impossible, that it was only a question of time, before the Roman Empire would come and crush it out of existence. According to all *a priori* probability the Religion of the Jews would disappear with their national existence,—and, as a matter of fact, many of the most characteristic features of Jewish religious life did disappear at the Destruction of Jerusalem and have never been renewed to this day. The Jewish State perished, but it left two daughters, Christianity and the Rabbinical Religion, which succeeded each in its own way in adapting its life to the new conditions.

I believe further that the faith of each of these descendants of ancient Judaism was justified by the result, different as the course of events turned out to be from what had been expected. The Christians expected the visible return of their Lord to judge the nations: they received instead the Roman Empire itself. They were justified in their expectation of a wholly new state of things, in their belief that the old state of things was worn out and ready to vanish away, and that in them alone were the seeds of life that were destined in due time to replenish the thought of the Western World. But for the venture of faith made by the early Christians, but for their belief in the New Age, the religion of Amos and Jeremiah would never have permeated the civilization of Europe. And those who believe in Religion believe that the faith of religious men in the obligations of right and wrong, and in the Power that makes for righteousness, is what keeps civilization alive, that makes it possible.

With this belief in the New Age the Christians naturally valued the books that told them of it. Their hope was in the future, the future just before them, in the Day of Judgement when the Son of Man would come and inaugurate the reign of the Saints. It was only when the vision faded away that these books fell out of favour. But by that time the Christian Church had struck root in new soil, in the Graeco-Roman civilization. It was living in the new world already, breathing the new air of Christian fellowship.

Let us turn now to the other side of the scene. The Christian movement did not attract the majority of the Jewish nation. Like other nations, like the English, the majority were disinclined to sacrifice everything for an ideal; there were doubtless many like the Rich Young Man in the Gospel, who was not willing to leave his great possessions and follow Jesus,—great possessions that he or his heir probably lost when the nation drifted into the disastrous war with Rome. Yet nothing would be more unjust than to regard the whole body of the Jews who did not become Christians as worldly or indifferent. There were others, and among them were some of the most deeply religious of the Jewish people, to whom the Christians seemed to be men who in ignorance were giving up the substance for the shadow. Israel was what it was by reason of God's Law, a Law sacred and divine in itself, the true interpretation of which had been handed down from generation to generation, an interpretation open to all who take the pains to learn it from those who had given their lives to its study. The Law of the Lord was a perfect Law, and it had been given to Israel to keep. It was a treasure-house of all wisdom: if any one be curious about the world to come, that which is fit for him to know about it may perhaps be found hidden in God's Law; if not, then it is probably an unsearchable secret. In any case, the first duty of an Israelite is to study the Law of his God, not to search in books of doubtful authenticity for the signs of the end of the world.

"The trivial round, the common task,
"Will furnish all we ought to ask,
"Room to deny ourselves,"—

(this last is a Christian phrase, is it not? Let us emend it for our present purposes into *Room to walk straighter yet*),

—"a road,
"To bring us daily nearer God."

I have ventured to use the language of the well-known Christian Hymn, in order that we may not forget that the frame of mind I am describing is eminently religious. It was an ideal of pious learning. I am not convinced that it was the dominant or the most popular ideal of religion in Israel during the first three-quarters of the first Christian century, during the period depicted in the Gospels. I should not be surprised, if during that exciting period the learned casuist may have often appeared dull and pedantic to the eager Apocalyptists, the half-heathen politicians, the fierce and uncompromising Zealots. The learned casuist could wait: his time was coming. When in the words of the Apocalypse of Baruch nothing was left save the Mighty One and His Law, the Rabbi was ready to guide his brethren along such of the old paths as still they were permitted to tread, and to shew them by precept and by example how to wait for the manifestation of the Sovereignty of God by taking upon themselves the Yoke and realising God's Sovereignty within them.

The work of the Rabbis, of Johanan ben Zakkai and his successors, was quietly heroic, and they succeeded so well in their reorganisation of Judaism that their work stands to this day. But—and it is here that the Apocalypses are directly concerned—they were able to carry their work through, just because they had dropped the conviction that had produced the Apocalypses. That is the reason why these Jewish documents, speaking generally, are preserved in Greek and not in Hebrew, by Christians and not by Jews.

I fear that I may seem to some of you to have wandered very far this evening from the proper province of Biblical Archaeology, and that some of my remarks may sound too vague and general, not to say homiletic, to be useful for the study of the ancient Apocalypses. But I am convinced that by far the most important thing for the student of these venerable documents, be he Jew or Christian, is to look at them from the right point of view, from the right historical point of view. They are not great in themselves. They are not worth much as literature, or as contributions to thought. They throw no light directly on the problems of our time, in the sense that Aeschylus or Plato, Amos or the Gospels, throw light. If one goes to the Apocalyptic literature for edification one does not get it. The most you arrive at is a sort of patronising approval for such elements as the ethical maxims in the Testaments of the Twelve Patriarchs.

No, the value of the Apocalypses is of quite a different order. They are the most characteristic survival of what I will venture to call, with all its narrowness and its incoherence, the heroic age of Jewish history, the age when the nation attempted to realise in action the part of the peculiar people of God. It ended in catastrophe, but the nation left two successors, the Christian Church and the Rabbinical Schools, each of which carried on some of the old national aims. And of the two it was the Christian Church that was most faithful to the ideas enshrined in the Apocalypses, and it did consider itself, not without some reason, the fulfilment of those ideas. What is wanted, therefore, in studying the Apocalypses is, above all, sympathy with the ideas that underlie them, and especially with the belief in the New Age. And those who believe that in Christianity a new Era really did dawn for us ought, I think, to have that sympathy.

What has happened to the Apocalypses is, after all, very much what has happened to the most striking external product of their age, I mean to the Maccabean Princes and the Martyrs through whose courage they rose to power. The Maccabeans proved in the end to be only worldly tyrants, and no one would gather from Talmudic sources how great a part they played in preserving Israel from a fatal penetration by Hellenic ideas. It is through the book called 1 Maccabees, preserved in Greek by the Christians, that we know of their heroic efforts. And the Martyrs, whose readiness to die for the faith was the bulwark of Israel's resistance, both passive and active, their fate is even harder. Their simple courage is enshrined in a wordy and rhetorical Greek tale, full of errors of fact and of taste. Yet in a very true sense it is on them that the foundation stone of the Christian movement was laid. They first set the example of Martyrdom, of passive resistance to what they could not actively prevent, for the sake of loyalty to an ideal. The oldest tale of these Martyrs is the story of Eleazar the aged priest and of the Woman with her seven sons, told in 2 Macc vi and vii. As I have just said, the tale as told there is wordy and rhetorical, and full of errors. Yet the historical investigator, who knows how heroic a movement is there represented and how far-reaching were its ultimate results, must regard the story with sympathy and some measure of respect. So also with the Apocalypses. They also are wordy, they contain errors of fact and of taste, and the New Age which they announce proved, when it came, to be different from what the Apocalyptists had anticipated. But we read them with sympathy when we think not only of the great movement which they heralded, but also of the unconquerable hope in the future to which they testify. We study the Apocalypses to learn how our spiritual ancestors hoped against hope that God would make all right in the end, and that we their children are here to-day studying them is an indication that their hope was not wholly unfounded.

II. THE BOOK OF ENOCH.

THE Book of Enoch is often referred to, but it is hardly so well known in fact as it ought to be, except to quite a small class of students. And indeed it is an odd and in some ways a not very attractive conglomeration. It is best therefore to begin at once with the prime reason that gives the book interest to us, and this is, its influence on the Christian Movement. 'Wandering Stars', we read in the Canonical Epistle of Jude, 'to these Enoch also, the seventh from Adam, prophesied, saying "Behold, the Lord came with ten thousands of His Holy ones to execute judgement upon all, and to convict all the ungodly of all their works of ungodliness which they have ungodly wrought, and of all the hard things which ungodly sinners have spoken against Him".'[1] This is a definite quotation which cannot be gainsaid. As a matter of fact, the words quoted are the last sentence of the opening paragraph of the Book of Enoch.[2] It is no mere illustration, no coincidence of ideas. 'Enoch' is quoted by name as inspired prophecy. This famous passage is very far from being the only trace of the influence of Enoch upon the New Testament, but it is the clearest and the best known. It is the best starting-point for our discussion of the book.

One thing may be noted at the outset. S. Jerome, in his account of Jude in *De Viris Illustribus*, says that inasmuch as in the Epistle a testimony is quoted from 'Enoch', an apocryphal Book, it is rejected by most. This unfavourable verdict has curiously persisted almost to our days in a different form. In the nineteenth century not so much stress was laid on canonicity as on date and authorship. Part of the reason that led some distinguished scholars to put the Epistle of Jude in the 2nd century A.D., and to question the right of its author to call himself the brother of James, was derived from the approval with which it seemed to stamp an 'apocryphal' writing. There was a widely-spread feeling that pure original Christianity must have been self-contained and rational, and in no sense based on unfamiliar and unhistorical Jewish legends. In a similar spirit the 'calmness' and 'sobriety' of the canonical Bible stories, both of the

[1] Jude 13–15.
[2] Enoch i 9 according to the modern chapters and verses.

Old and New Testaments, were very often contrasted with the 'extravagance' of uncanonical 'fables'.

I well know that I am now touching upon a large and very thorny subject, into which it is not the province of these Lectures to go. My chief object in mentioning it here is to remark that this view does not carry us very far when we are tracing back popular beliefs and popular enthusiasms to their earliest forms. The one thing quite certain about the early Christians is that they were enthusiasts; those who joined them joined because they were enthusiasts, and the first expression of their hopes and fears were unrestrained and sometimes crude. The early Christians were 'full of new wine'. We are more likely to find bad literary and historical criticism in an 'early' Christian document than a 'late' one: 'moderation' is likely to be the mark of the second generation rather than the first, and certainly the respect paid in the Epistle of Jude to the Book of Enoch is no reason for putting that Epistle late. In the next Lecture we shall see that something similar may be said about the date of the Christian Apocalypse called the Ascension of Isaiah.

To return to 'Enoch', it must be frankly confessed that the mode of quotation in Jude does imply that the writer of the Epistle believed that the Book of Enoch was the work of the Patriarch. It would be a very interesting subject to investigate to what extent the reputed authorship of pseudonymous books actually secured or influenced their reception in ancient times. What is certain is that when they were rejected it was on grounds of doctrine rather than of historical scepticism, although we may gather from Tertullian that some people did wonder how the Book of Enoch escaped the Flood.[1] But there is another aspect of pseudonymous authorship to which I venture to think sufficient attention has not been given. It is this, that the names were not chosen out of mere caprice; they indicated to a certain extent what subjects would be treated and the point of view of the writer.

For example, there is the Apocalypse of Baruch. The historical Baruch lived in the days of Nebuchadnezzar. Consequently in his Apocalypse he is supposed to be acquainted with the names of the personages who figure in the pre-exilic history of Israel. But though

[1] My friend Mr G. R. S. Mead has reminded me that this question was also considered by those who received other 'writings' of Enoch, as appears from the Gnostic work *Pistis Sophia* 354, according to which the "Books of Ieu" were deposited by Enoch in the rock of Ararat and miraculously preserved there from the Flood by a 'Ruler' superior to Fate. In the Book of Enoch itself Enoch gives his teaching quite openly to Methuselah, e. g. lxxxiii 1, lxxxv 2.

the real interest of the author is in the fate of the Jews after the Destruction of Jerusalem by Titus, 'Baruch' mentions no one by name later than the day of the historical Baruch. In the Assumption of Moses, given out as the last dying-speech of Moses to Joshua but really dating from about 9 A. D., the history of Israel is sketched in figurative though quite comprehensible terms. But no name is mentioned. As I once wrote elsewhere,[1] the Seers of old are supposed to foretell *events* and to understand *doctrines*, but they must be silent about *names*. Daniel may predict the wars of the successors of Alexander, and in chap. xi we can even follow the details of their campaigns, but he must not mention the names of Antiochus and Ptolemy, of Antioch and Alexandria. If he needs to announce the coming of the great over-sea Power from the West, he must not mention the Romans, for the name was unknown in the days of Belshazzar; he must speak of the ships of Chittim.[2]

But further, the choice of a name shews more or less what problems occupy the writer's mind. Baruch and Ezra were Jews in the strict sense of the word, members of the organized historical Jewish Church-Nation, men to whom no sacrifice was valid outside Jerusalem. Their outlook is the strictly Jewish outlook, God is to them above all things the God of the Chosen People, the problems dealt with are concerned with the fortunes of the Chosen People. And so in the books which bear their names the consummation of all things is found in the Messianic Kingdom. The outlook is national. How different from this is the Book of Job! Here the scene is laid in patriarchal times and the place is somewhere far away in the East. Why? Because the writer, who I do not doubt was also a strict Jew, wished to speak about some of the problems of human life apart from the individualities of Jewish customs, divinely enjoined though they might be.

So it is with the Book of Enoch. Enoch was the great-great-grandfather of Shem, but he was the great-great-grandfather of Ham and Japhet too. What was Enoch's nationality? He might appropriately reply *Homo sum*, and accordingly no spot on the wide earth is alien from him, though its centre is still Jerusalem. In the course of his long book there occurs a Vision of the history of mankind, in which the centre of interest is, of course, the fortunes of the Chosen People, but elsewhere the outlook is to a certain extent cosmopolitan. The Sun and the Moon and the Stars, about which Enoch has so much to tell us, shine equally on Jew and Gentile. And the theme of the first part of the work, the Origin of Evil, has (alas!) equal interest for all

[1] *Journ. of Theol. Studies* xiii 374.

[2] See Dan xi 30.

races. The writer was surely an orthodox Jew and his book was written for his countrymen to read, but like the Book of Job it is concerned with mankind and the world inhabited by mankind as a whole; it attempts to "justify the ways of God to men", and not only His dealings with the custodians of His Revelation in Judaea.

The contents of the Book of Enoch are, very roughly, as follows:—

After a short Prelude, which strikes the dominant note of the whole literature with its announcement of impending Judgement (i–v), we are told the story of how the 'Watchers', i.e. the Angels, sons of God, came down to earth and married the daughters of Men, thereby bringing all sorts of evil on mankind, first, because their offspring were Giants who devoured men and crops, and secondly, because the Arts and the Sciences were taught by the Watchers to their wives and to the other human beings with whom they came in contact (vi–viii). The leaders of the Watchers were named Semiaza and Azael (or Azazel). Moved by the cry of men suffering under the horrors of Civilization, the Most High interferes. Azael and his companions are to be punished and the earth is to be cleansed by the Flood, and only the son of Lamech, i.e. Noah, is to escape, so that mankind may be started afresh from his descendants (ix–xi).

Before all this had happened Enoch had been taken to live a kind of life between earth and heaven. It was he who had been deputed to announce the Divine Sentence against Azael. Azael appeals for mercy, and Enoch prepares and presents Azael's petition before the Most High, but it fails: Azael is reduced to impotence for ever and his monstrous offspring become the demons in the air all round us (xii–xvi).

Enoch is then taken by holy Angels to view the world from the West to the East (xvii–xxxvi). He sees everything, even to Chaos and beyond Earth and Heaven. He sees also the deep Valleys where the spirits of the dead will be kept till the Day of Judgement (xxii).[1]

Here ends the First Book. The Second, called the *Parables* or *Similitudes* of Enoch, contains Enoch's visions of the pre-existent Elect Messiah, often called in this section 'the Son of Man', who at

[1] The description is somewhat difficult to follow in parts, because the transmitted text is full of small errors. But it appears that of the four Valleys one will be sufficient to contain the spirits of the righteous: this Valley is bright and there is a fountain of water in it (xxii 2). One of the four Valleys is apparently reserved for those who are neither righteous nor definitely wicked, like Kipling's Tomlinson, and like Tomlinson they fail to attain either to Heaven or to Hell (xxii 13). For the text, see Appendix I.

the appointed time will judge the Kings and the mighty rulers of the earth and vindicate the oppressed righteous. In this section God is generally called the 'Lord of Spirits,' (xxxvii–lxxi).

The Third Book is astronomical, and teaches that the year has, or should have, 364 days (lxxii–lxxxii).

The Fourth Book contains Enoch's Vision of Israelite history, which ends some time during the Maccabean period (lxxxiii–xci). This is followed by admonitions and somewhat vague prophecies of the future (xcii–cv). At the end comes an Appendix about the birth of Noah, only loosely connected with what goes before (cvi–cviii).

Such are the contents of the Book, or rather the Books, of Enoch. There is reported in the Talmud a saying of Rabbi Aḳiba, to the effect that he who reads outside, i.e. non-canonical, books is like a man reading a letter that has no sense. I think that those of you who have tried to read 'Enoch' will agree that the first impression it leaves is that of words with very little sense. The Greeks called the universe the *Cosmos*, meaning thereby an ordered whole; 'Enoch' is the most unhellenic of writings, and seems to be dominated by the very Spirit of Chaos, if there be such a thing.

Nevertheless it is an attempt to see the world steadily and to see it whole, to unify the physical world, the moral world, and the political world, the world, that is, of the national destiny of God's chosen People. It contains a serious attempt to account for the presence of Evil in human history, and this attempt claims our attention, because it is in essentials the view presupposed in the Gospels, especially the Synoptic Gospels. It is when you study Matthew, Mark and Luke against the background of the Books of Enoch that you see them in their true perspective.

In saying this I have no intention of detracting from the importance of what the Gospels report to us. On the contrary, it puts familiar words into their proper setting. Indeed it seems to me that some of the best-known Sayings of Jesus only appear in their true light if regarded as *Midrash* upon words and concepts taken from Enoch, words and concepts that were familiar to those who heard the Prophet of Galilee, though now they have been forgotten by Jew and Christian alike.

An instance of what I mean is to be found in the Saying about the Unclean Spirit reported in Matt xii 43–45, Lk xi 24–26. "The unclean spirit", said Jesus once, "when it is gone out of the man passes through waterless places, seeking rest and finding none; then it says 'To my house I will return from whence I came forth,' and on coming finds it swept and garnished. Then it goes and takes with it seven others worse than itself and they enter and dwell there—and the last state of that man becomes worse than the first." Matt xii 44 adds that it was empty as well as swept and garnished, and when the Saying is used in the pulpit most of the weight is usually made to fall on this addition, though I doubt whether it be more than a gloss added by the Evangelist to bring out the assumed sense. In any case the passage is treated as a sort of revelation about what may be called the Natural History of demons and demoniacs, as so much information given. That I am sure is wrong; the Saying does not give information at all. It simply assumes the then popular belief about demoniacs and the cause of their affliction, a belief which is set forth at length in Enoch, chapter xv. There we read that the demons are the progeny of the heavenly Sons of God and the Daughters of men. They are 'spirit' like their fathers, but they cannot rise far from the surface of the earth, the home of their mothers, and they are evil, "oppressive, destroying, attacking, wrestling, casting men upon the ground,[1] making them run mad, spirits that can eat nothing but fast all the time and thirst and dash themselves about. And these attack the sons of men and women, because they have come forth from them." It is the same doctrine as is presupposed in the Gospel; the unclean demons are about in the air, seeking rest and finding none except in a human body. But if you look at the context in the Gospel, you will find that the point of the Saying of Jesus is not to give information about the demons, but to draw a comparison between what was commonly believed about the recurring attacks suffered by a 'demoniac' and the state of mind of the Jewish people. "So will it be also to this evil generation", said Jesus according to Matthew, and whether this part of the Saying be authentic reminiscence or an interpretation of what has gone before, it certainly hits the general meaning. "It is by no pact with the powers of evil", says Jesus in effect, "that I exorcise unclean spirits from those you bring to me; I am neither setting forth a new doctrine nor practising new and unlawful methods. If I can do good to men because the 'spirit' that is with me is the spirit of God, it shews you the Kingdom of God at your doors before you were aware of it (ἔφθασεν ἐφ' ὑμᾶσ). The power of God is with me, stronger than the powers of evil (Matt xii 26–29, Lk xi 18–22). Which side will you take? (Matt xii 30, Lk xi 23). Blessed are they that hear the word of God and also keep it: you hear the word now; take care that presently you do not lose it again, like a man who has been set

[1] Compare the description of the demoniac in Mk ix 20.

free from the dominion of the Evil One, but afterwards is taken possession of once more. If you neglect to take my message to heart, your last state will be worse than it was before you listened to it (Matt xii 43–45, Lk xi 24–28)."

The Gospel Saying about the restless wandering spirit implies the same view of aerial demons and their nature as is expressly set forth in 'Enoch'. In fact the aim of the first section of Enoch (vi–xvi) is to explain how the demons come to be in the air and why they attack men. At the same time the evidence with regard to the Saying that we have just considered is quite inadequate to prove a literary use of our Book of Enoch. All that can strictly be concluded is that the same doctrine forms the background in the Gospel and in Enoch. The case is different with regard to the Judgement scene in Enoch lxii and Matt xxv. Here I venture to think that the Similitudes of Enoch are presupposed in the scene from Matthew, in the same way as the Vision of Daniel is presupposed in all the passages that speak about the Son of Man coming with the clouds of heaven. And just the same mistake is generally made by Christian commentators about Matt xxv 31–46 as they make about the Saying concerning the aerial demon, that is, an attempt is made to extract positive teaching out of what is merely presupposed and assumed.

But first let us put the two passages together. The Similitudes of Enoch contain the visions of the patriarch concerning the Son of Man. There is not much doubt about the origin of the phrase in Enoch: the name and the general conception is taken from Dan vii, though what in Daniel had been little more than a symbol for the Jewish Nation is in Enoch a personal heavenly being. In chap. xlvi the Son of Man is with the Ancient of Days, Whose Head is white like wool, i.e. with the Most High as described in Dan vii 9. Enoch is told that the Son of Man is the one who hath righteousness, with whom dwelleth righteousness, whom the Lord of Spirits hath chosen, whose function is in God's good time to judge the kings and mighty ones that now possess the earth. A vision of this Judgement is granted to Enoch (chap. lxii): "The Lord of Spirits seated the Elect One on the throne of his glory and the spirit of righteousness was poured out before him . . . And there will stand up in that day all the kings and the mighty and the exalted and those who hold the earth, and they will see and recognise him how he sits on the throne of his glory and righteousness is judged before him and no lying word is spoken before him, . . . and one portion of them will look on the other and they will be terrified and their countenance will fall and pain will seize them when they see that Son of Man sitting on the throne of his glory, . . . and all the elect will stand before him on that day. And all the kings and the mighty . . . will supplicate for mercy at his hand. Nevertheless . . . the angels of punishment will take them in charge to execute vengeance upon them, because they have oppressed his children and his elect. And they will be a spectacle for the righteous and for his elect, . . . and the righteous and elect will be saved on that day . . . and the Lord of Spirits will abide over them and with that Son of Man will they eat and lie down and rise up for ever and ever." The kings and the mighty pray for a respite but cannot obtain it, and they say: "Our souls are filled with the mammon of unrighteousness, but this does not prevent us from descending into the flame of the pain of Sheol" (lxiii 10).

Let me remind you of the words of the parallel passage in Matt xxv: "When the Son of Man shall come in his glory and all the angels with him, then shall he sit on the throne of his glory, and before him shall be gathered all the nations, and he shall separate them as the shepherd separateth the sheep from the goats, and he shall set the sheep on his right hand and the goats on his left. Then shall the King say unto them on his right hand, 'Come ye blessed of my Father, inherit the kingdom prepared for you from the foundation of the world, for I was hungry and ye gave me meat, I was thirsty and ye gave me drink, I was a stranger and ye took me in, naked and ye clothed me, sick and ye visited me, in prison and ye came unto me'." You know how it goes on: how the 'righteous' declare that they do not know when they had had the opportunity of succouring the Lord of the Day of Judgement, and they are told that what they had done to one of the least of His brethren they had done unto Him; and then how those on the left are sent away into the fire prepared for the devil and his angels, because inasmuch as they had not done it unto the least of the King's brethren they had not done it unto Him.

It is surely impossible not to recognise a real literary connexion between these pictures of the Judgement. In both we read of 'the Son of Man' who 'sits on the throne of his glory', in both the 'righteous' get their vindication and reward, while the adversaries to their surprise are banished to flame and torment. The one picture is evidently an adaptation of the other, and the question arises which is the pattern and which the copy. It is not a question of the comparative merits of the two pieces. The passage in the Gospel of Matthew is magnificent as literature. The picture is sketched in very few strokes, yet every one of them tells, the four-fold enumeration of the works of mercy (shortened at each repetition) giving a kind of rhythmical swing to the narration, that lifts it at once out of the sphere of material description into that of epic poetry. The scene in Enoch, on the other hand, is confused and laboured, and it is not enlivened by grace either of style or thought. It deals with the most awful events that the human mind can contemplate in the spirit of plain prose.

But when we pass from considerations of value to considerations of priority there can be little doubt that Enoch is the original. It is just one of those cases where S. Paul's canon applies: "howbeit that is not first which is spiritual, but that which is natural, and afterward that which is spiritual." The description of the Judgement in Enoch is complete in itself; it is the imagined end of the kingdoms of the world, whose rulers are judged for their failure to discover and pay homage to the True God (lxiii 4, 7–9). In a word, they are condemned for being Gentiles. This is a natural view for a Jewish Seer to take at a time when his people are still palpitating with the life and death struggle against the powers of Hellenism. There is indeed evidence that so summary an Assize was felt in some quarters to be unjust, and in the Apocalypse of Baruch it is only those who have ruled over Israel, or have had dealings with them, that are given up to the sword; the nations which knew not Israel and have not trodden down the seed of Jacob will be spared—they are needed, because some out of every nation will be subjected to the Israelites (*Apoc. Bar.* lxxii 4–6).

In the Gospel the Gentiles are judged by the kindness they have shewn to the persecuted brethren of the Son of Man. Obviously this is a very imperfect test, inasmuch as the greater part of the Gentiles would have had no dealings with them at all. It seems to me therefore that we are really in the presence of a sort of *Midrash*, by which I mean an application of the Judgement-scene in Enoch to enforce a particular moral. We do Matt xxv 31 ff. an injustice if we treat it as a description of the Day of Judgement given to an audience who did not know beforehand what would happen there: on the contrary, it assumes that the scene of Judgement as given in Enoch is already familiar, and then goes on to tell the well-known tale again—with a difference.

In any case I must regard the Similitudes of Enoch as having consciously supplied the framework for the scene in Matthew. It is because the Book of Enoch does thus stand behind the Gospels that it is of such importance to the Christian student.

I must now say a few words about the transmission of the Book of Enoch and even touch upon certain details of the text, because what I have in mind is concerned with the important question of the nationality of the writer. Apart from a few quotations our knowledge of the text of Enoch comes from four sources.

1. The whole work is preserved in Ethiopic, forming an integral part of the Old Testament as received by the Abyssinian Church. This Ethiopic text is a fairly literal translation from the Greek, made apparently in the 4th century, in the early days of Ethiopic Christianity. There are many MSS of it extant, but they all go back to the same translation, so that the value of the Ethiopic text, where we can retranslate it with certainty back into Greek, is that of a single ancient Greek MS.[1]

2. A vellum MS now at the Cairo Museum (formerly at Gizeh), discovered in 1886 and probably of the 6th century, contains Enoch i 1–xxxii 6, i.e. about the first third of the whole.

3. A miscellaneous MS in the Vatican (*Vat. Gr.* 1809) contains Enoch lxxxix 42–49 in Greek shorthand. This small fragment was thus preserved as a reading exercise; its importance consists in the fact that such an excerpt must have been taken originally from a continuous text, and lessens the probability that the Cairo text only contained the First Part, without the Similitudes.

4. Georgius the Syncellus, a chronographical writer of the 8th century, quotes Enoch vi 1–ix 4, viii 4–x 14, xv 8–xvi 1.

These last, the extracts from the Syncellus, were for a long time the only portions of the Book of Enoch known. It was natural therefore that editors of the Ethiopic translation should have regarded the passages where the Ethiopic differs from the Syncellus as due to the nature of a translation or to the clumsiness of the translator. And when the Cairo Greek MS turned up and was found in many places to agree with the Ethiopic, Dr. Charles still holds to the general superiority of the Syncellus extracts and has maintained that the Ethiopic and the Cairo MS belong to a special recension or type of text which is, according to him, often inferior to the extracts. I feel bound therefore to give some reasons for regarding the Cairo MS as better, and for treating the extracts given by the Syncellus as to a certain degree sophisticated.

In the first place this is only what we might expect. The Cairo MS was written by unintelligent mechanical scribes, men who may leave out lines and make mistakes, but who do not seem to have made intentional alterations. The chronographer, on the other hand, only brings in his extracts to illustrate his work: he regards Enoch

[1] The Ethiopic text has been admirably edited by R. H. Charles (Oxford, 1906), who gives also the Greek Fragments in full.

as 'Apocrypha', not as sacred, and was under no obligation to refrain from casual emendations. It is therefore not surprising to find that in quoting Enoch vii 1 the Syncellus has interpolated his own chronology into the text and in xvi 1 he has brought in a gloss about the 'Nephilim';[1] while in viii 4, where the true text has simply 'so the cry of perishing mankind came up to heaven', the Syncellus gives us in two places two different versions of the cry.[2]

The Cairo MS is certainly not written with much intelligence. The first scribe began in the middle of Enoch, at xix 3, in the middle of a sentence. He went on then to xxi 9, where he breaks off and begins at i 1, in the middle of a line, without any indication that the text is disturbed. No doubt his exemplar had a leaf loose which had been placed in front of the text, but it is odd to find the intelligence of the scribe so small as not to know where the book he is copying begins. As we might expect after this, his standard of accuracy is low; he leaves out sentences here and there, often making havoc of the sense. But at least he makes no intentional changes, and where his text makes any sense at all it seems to me that we do safest to follow it.[3]

After all, the Greek is itself a translation, not an original. This is maintained by almost all those who have worked at Enoch, though further proofs of acquaintance with Palestine are sometimes asked for by Jewish scholars. What is chiefly in dispute is whether the work was originally written in Hebrew or Aramaic. It might be thought that such a question could be definitely settled at once, but unfortunately this is not the case, and most of the most convincing proofs that the Greek text of Enoch is a translation from a Semitic language fit equally well with a Hebrew or an Aramaic original. Thus in Enoch x 17 the Greek has *τὰ σάββατα αὐτῶν*, where the context shews that the original had 'their old age'. Assuming that this original was in Aramaic, this implies that the translator had שבתהון before him, but that he read it *shabbatthōn* (שַׁבַּתְּהוֹן) instead of *sēbuthhōn* (שֵׂבְתְהוֹן). But the letters of the corresponding Hebrew word שבתם could equally well be read either way.

My own opinion is that the original language of Enoch was Aramaic, but that a few passages do seem to suggest a Hebrew origin, yet not decisively. Certainly the question will never be settled by arguments based on ingenious jingles or *paronomasiae* in conjecturally

[1] See the Notes to Charles's edition, who recognises these additions as editorial glosses by Syncellus.

[2] Here Charles most incomprehensibly maintains that the Syncellus text is original. But which text?

[3] See further, Appendix I.

restored Semitic originals. We must be sure that the jingle was in the original at all, before we can draw any safe arguments from it.

The nationality of the author of Enoch has to be inferred from the knowledge of geography and topography which he displays. What makes inference difficult is that he writes in the person of a Patriarch who lived before the Deluge and the Tower of Babel, so that he is debarred from using any names of cities or towns. In his aerial journeys he visits the site of Jerusalem (xxvi f.) and looks down into the Valley of Jehoshaphat, where the Judgement will take place, but no name is mentioned, only that it is the centre of the earth. That, however, was a belief which might have been held by a Jew wherever he lived. The topography of the stream of Siloam and the Mount of Olives is correct, but here again it might be said that the author knew Jerusalem because he had attended the Feasts. More striking is the fact that in Enoch x 4 f. the decree goes forth that Azael (or Azazel—both forms occur) is to be cast "into the desert which is in Dudael" (or Daduel), and to have rough and jagged rocks placed upon him. This seems to indicate a knowledge that the scape-goat 'for Azazel' in Lev xvi 10 was sent to die in a hard and rough place called Beth Hadudo, i.e. it shews some acquaintance with ritual as actually practised in the Holy Land.

But the place where the author of Enoch seems most at home is the head-waters of the Jordan. Here, and here only, he breaks his rule of naming no names. When the fallen Sons of God entrust Enoch with their petition he goes off and sits down at the Waters of Dan in the land of Dan (xiii 7). This is a perfectly definite place, the most northerly town in Israel, familiar to us in the phrase 'from Dan to Beersheba'. Whether we identify it with the modern Banias or the modern Tell-el-Ḳādi, it is equally a main source of the Jordan. The author of Enoch, as you see, knows that there are 'waters' there, and he adds, quite correctly, that it is south-west of Mount Hermon, the hill upon which the Watchers descended when they came to earth.

But this is not all. The Watchers seem to have haunted this region as long as they could, for when Enoch awakes from his Visions and goes to find them, they are sitting gathered together weeping in Abelsiael,[1] which is between Lebanon and Seniser.[2] The last word is evidently a scribe's corruption for Senir, the other name for Hermon (Deut iii 9), or for a part of it (Cant iv 8): the place was therefore in the valley between the two great ranges of mountains. And here,

[1] So the Ethiopic. The Cairo MS has ϹΕΝΕΒΕΛϹΑΤΑ, which I suppose is miswritten for ΕΝ ΑΒΕΛ Ϲ[Ι]ΑΛ[Α].

[2] Enoch xiii 9: the Cairo MS has ϹΕΝΙϹΗΛ.

THE JORDAN VALLEY AND ITS SOURCES

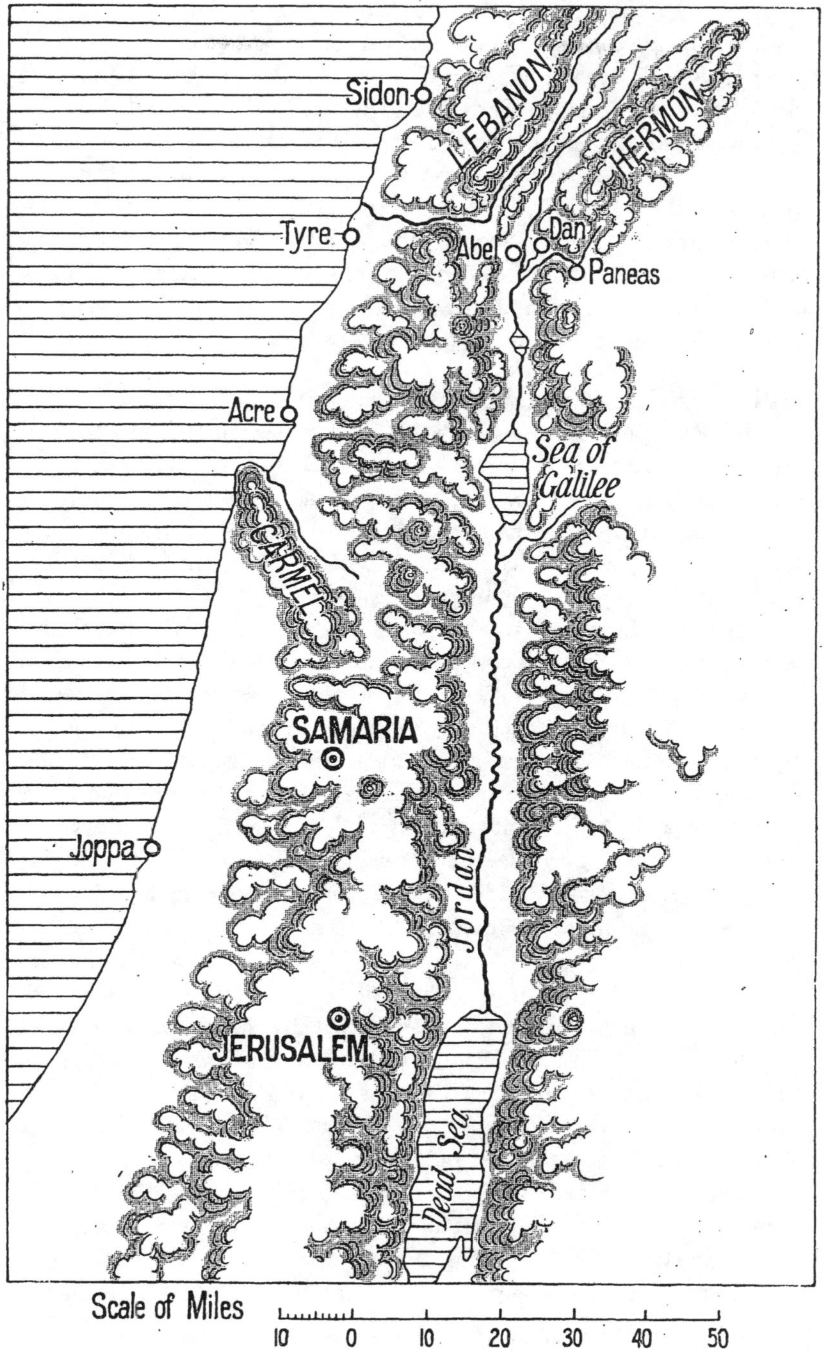

as a matter of fact, quite close to the Waters of Dan, we find the town Abel, called also Abel of Beth-Ma'acha to distinguish it from other towns of the same name. The name really means 'meadow' or 'lea', but it happens to be very much like a Hebrew and Aramaic word which means 'mourning' or 'weeping', and so it seemed to be an appropriate spot for the weeping Sons of God. In old times, as we know, 'they were wont to ask in Abel' (2 Sam xx 18); this seems to refer to some ancient legend, and it is just possible that an early form of the Enoch-Saga may have belonged to that region. In any case it is the country round the sources of the Jordan that seems to be most familiar to the author of our Book of Enoch.[1]

I have dwelt thus at length upon the personality of the author of Enoch because of the importance of any evidence which tends to shew that it is really a Palestinian book, one therefore which circulated among Jews in Palestine. If moreover the author came from the north, that helps to explain the influence the book had upon the Religion that was cradled in Galilee. It is now time to consider something of the general message of Enoch.

In the last Lecture I tried to make the Apocalyptic Hope clearer by contrasting with it the religious ideal of the Rabbis by whom it was rejected. As a contrast to 'Enoch', if I may use this name for the author or authors of the Book of Enoch, let me invite you to glance at the imposing figure of the eclectic philosopher Posidonius. In many ways there is a striking likeness between the two. To begin with, they are almost contemporary and almost fellow-countrymen. In the year 135 B.C., the year in which John Hyrcanus began his long and prosperous reign, Posidonius was born at Apamea, a Syrian city about a hundred miles north of the sources of the Jordan. He died in 51 B.C. at the age of 84. Enoch and Posidonius have further this in common, that it is only in recent times modern scholars have recognised their importance as representative of the age in which they lived. It is in the person of Posidonius, we are told, that the heathen Philosopher became a Prophet of Religion[2]; through Posidonius, more than any other man, was effected that fusion of Oriental religions and Greek speculation which gave birth to the Western Mysteries of Isis and of Mithra, to the cult of the Sun and the Planets that survives in our names for the days of the week, and, more important than all, to the Natural Religion of cultivated men under the Empire, to the creeds of Seneca, of Plutarch, of Marcus

[1] For the reference in Enoch vi 6 to the same stretch of country, see Appendix I.
[2] Reitzenstein, *Die Hellenistischen Mysterienreligionen*, p. 5.

Aurelius. Perhaps not all of this can be strictly substantiated. Still it is fair to say that Posidonius was as truly a formative influence on pagan culture as Enoch was on Christianity.

There are further resemblances between the two figures we are contrasting. Both alike are interested in the Universe as a whole. Posidonius really did travel in some of those remote regions of the North and West which Enoch describes. He was interested in all natural phenomena, but, as with Enoch, his special interest was in the heavens, these heavens above us, in which the Sun and Moon have their course. And below the Moon, in the sublunary sphere, to Posidonius as to Enoch, the air was full of demons, beings whose substance was lighter than flesh and blood, but yet too gross to ascend into the empyrean.

We read Enoch to get the mental background of the apostles and of the crowds that listened to our Lord, and when we find this background strange and barbarous we must remember that the world as imagined by the most cultivated and learned folk of that time was also strange and different from what we have learned now to believe about it. But there are greater differences between Posidonius and Enoch than details of cosmology. They differed in their view of the purpose of the world, and therefore they differed in the message they had to deliver.

In an illuminating sketch of Posidonius, which some of you may have been reading lately, Mr Edwyn Bevan has summed up the philosopher's aim as an attempt "to make men at home in the Universe"[1]. This was not the aim of Enoch. The world which was set forth in the philosophy of Posidonius had many features in common with the world of Enoch, but Enoch's world was not an end in itself. Enoch tells us of the world, to shew us that everything in it is prepared for the inevitable Judgement of the Most High. Even the stars that failed to rise at their appointed times have a place of punishment at the extremity of heaven and earth.[2] The angels that transgressed will be judged by God, so will the men who have followed the teachings of these angels. The spirits of the dead wait in their remote enclosures until the great Day, the Day which will witness the transvaluation of all values, when the afflicted Saints are vindicated and the Kings and the Mighty ones of the earth are brought low.

There is no great Day in the world of Posidonius. There is no Hell either: "the only real hell was found here on this earth and the

[1] E. Bevan, *Stoics and Sceptics* (Oxford, 1913), p. 98. Most of what I have to say about Posidonius is taken from this admirable book.

[2] Enoch xviii 13 ff., xxi 6: see the Note at the end of Appendix I, p. 70.

impure were ever drawn back into it anew."[1] The impure were tied to their earthly body: the body, the tomb of the rational spirit (*sōma—sēma*),—that was the underlying formula. And so the light and purified souls of good men ascend to the heavens and, as Mr Bevan puts it, following Seneca and Cicero, watch the stars go round: *felix qui potuit rerum cognoscere causas.*[2] And when you knew the causes of things, what did you see? What was the world in which you learned to be at home? After all, it was a dull affair, like a glass of muddy water, in which the only effective motion was the slow settling down of the sediment towards the bottom.

This was the world that Israel refused to accept. The rarefied air of the Stoic heaven was one in which the Jew did not easily breathe—and small blame to him. He demanded an ultimate reward for his labour, even at the price of punishment for his faults: otherwise the world seemed to him meaningless. And so, when the Jew does contemplate the world as a whole, as is done in Enoch, it is all placed under the eye of God, who made it, and whose Judgement upon it will give it its meaning. In construction, in its denizens, it is very much like the world of Posidonius, but it does not exist for itself. "Be hopeful," says Enoch to the righteous, "aforetime ye have been put to shame through evil and affliction, but now ye shall shine as the lights of heaven. . . . Fear not, when ye see the sinners growing strong and prospering in their ways: be not companions with them, but keep afar from their violence; for ye shall become companions of the hosts of heaven."[3] Yes, but this glorious future does not come κατὰ φύσιν, according to Nature, according to the inevitable course of things we see around us. It comes because the names of the righteous are written in the presence of the glory of the Most High.[4]

In the last resort the difference between Posidonius and Enoch, between late Hellenic Civilization and the Jews that refused to be dominated by it, is symbolized in the sentence from 4 Ezra, which says directly and in so many words "The Most High hath not made one world, but two".[5] This is the essential thing, the central doctrine that animates all the Apocalypses. In one sense it is a confession of failure, a confession that the Universe cannot be reduced to a harmonious whole. Posidonius professed to do this, but he and his followers only achieved it by denying the existence of evil in the world.

I am not a philosopher and I do not believe that philosophy, or indeed reflexion in general, is really creative. Instinct and conviction, often inarticulate, are creative, and man uses his powers of thought

[1] Bevan, p. 109. [2] pp. 111, 112. [3] Enoch civ 2, 6.
[4] Enoch civ 1. [5] 4 Ezra vii 50.

and reflexion to justify the actions to which his instincts and convictions have led him. So I do not imagine that either Enoch or Posidônius moved the minds of men, but they reflected them like a mirror. The Macedonian Empire had once for all put an end to the old city-states of Greece and the wonderful progressive development of the human spirit that they had fostered. In Asia the conquests of Alexander had acted as a solvent upon the old religions of the East. East and West flowed together, under new political conditions. The result was a new semi-Greek semi-Oriental civilization, which after a few generations became articulate and systematic in Posidonius and his followers. This civilization was rejected by one people, the Jews, who clung with passionate loyalty to the God of their fathers. They believed Him to be the only true God, and consequently that in the end He would not desert them in their struggle to maintain His worship and His sacred Law. It was the action of the Jews that produced the Apocalyptists, just as the actions of Alexander the Great were the real makers of Posidonius and his philosophy. The promises and warnings in Enoch give articulate expression to the impulses that moved the Jews to die rather than let their ancestral Religion be assimilated to that of the Gentiles.

And those who cling to the belief that human history is not altogether meaningless and that it marches, however slowly and haltingly, to a definite goal ought to regard the ideas enshrined in books like Enoch with sympathy. It is by this doctrine of a purpose underlying history, and of an unerring Judgement to be pronounced upon it somewhen, somewhere, that these books still strike a chord in our hearts to-day. But their main value was as an encouragement for their contemporaries, to nerve the Jews to continue the struggle for the national ideals, which their instincts had led them to begin. Some of the Apocalypses, like Daniel, must have been first issued at moments of crisis; others, like Enoch, may have seen the light at calmer and more prosperous seasons, when the Apocalyptist could extend his outlook over the whole known Universe and consider mankind in general. Such times were perhaps more dangerous for the Jewish ideals than moments of open persecution; at such times we can see most clearly that the true antagonists are not King Antiochus and the Maccabees but the 'scientific' and the 'religious' view of the world and of human fate. Enoch has the faults of a pioneer. His work is rough, he is unacquainted with the country, he often loses his way. But his guiding star is a belief that the confused drama of History is not without a purpose, and that in the end the Judge of all the Earth can and will do right.

III. THE MINOR JEWISH APOCALYPSES.

An adequate treatment of the problems raised by the minor Jewish Apocalypses would require a long course of Lectures, and I shall not attempt to cover the ground in a single discourse. My aim rather is to bring out certain points of interest from these writings, which more or less illustrate what I have already said in the two former lectures about the Apocalyptic Idea and the Book of Enoch.

The first work to claim our attention is the *Testaments of the Twelve Patriarchs*. Perhaps the most remarkable and interesting feature in this work is its title, or rather I should say, its general scope and plan. The *Testaments* profess to be the last dying speeches and admonitions of the ancestors of the Twelve Tribes of Israel, Reuben, Simeon, Levi, &c., to their immediate descendants. Here at once we have a problem. We ask 'for whom was the work intended?' What special interest have the sayings of Reuben or Naphtali for the Jews of the Maccabean age? We all know that the Ten Tribes had gone into captivity centuries ago. What, then, was the point of writing in the name of their eponymous ancestors?

The answer to this question is found in the contents of the work, which contains internal evidence of its original date. Much as I differ from Dr. Charles's somewhat fanciful theories about the MS transmission of the *Testaments*, I am glad to be in full agreement with him in his general view of the work, which he places during the prosperous reign of John Hyrcanus, nephew of Judas Maccabaeus. The insistence upon the future glories of Levi fit nothing in history but the Asmonaean dynasty. To quote Dr. Charles himself (§ 14, p. xlii): "Reuben admonishes his sons 'To Levi draw near in lowliness of your heart, that ye may receive a blessing from his mouth, for him hath the Lord chosen to reign before all the people' (*R* vi 10). Here a High-priest who is also a king is referred to. Such a combination of offices naturally makes us think of the Maccabean Priest-kings of the second century B.C. The possibility of doubting this reference is excluded by the words that immediately follow: 'and ye shall do obeisance to his seed, for on your account it shall die in wars both seen and unseen; and among you it shall be king for ever.' Thus the High-priest is not only a high-priest and civil ruler, but also a warrior.

That the Maccabean high-priests are here designed cannot be reasonably doubted."[1]

What I wish to bring out is that the political conditions of the reign of John Hyrcanus give point to the choice of the Twelve Patriarchs as the speakers in the book. The realm of John Hyrcanus was extensive. For the first time since Solomon an Israelite monarch was ruling over the whole of the Promised Land. But who were the inhabitants of his dominions? In Judaea, of course, and above all in the district round Jerusalem, there were the Jews *pur sang*, the unmixed descendants of the returned Exiles. But who were the Samaritans that lived in Samaria? Who were the inhabitants of the region beyond Jordan? And who, towards the end of the 2nd century B.C., were the Galileans?

The answer to these questions involves a good deal of ancient and recent history and, as in most ethnological questions, it is fairly easy to produce a plausible case for directly opposite conclusions. On the one hand it may be urged that the inhabitants of Galilee and the other outlying dominions of Hyrcanus were not Israelites at all. In 1 Macc v 23, 45 ff., we read how Judas Maccabaeus and his brother Simon collected the loyal Israelites from Gilead, i.e. Peraea, and from Galilee, and brought them with their wives and children to Judaea. Thus, whatever may have been the state of things before this, all the Holy Land was denuded of Israelites except Judaea itself. A generation later the victorious Jews occupy the surrounding territories. A great movement of religious proselytism is then set on foot: the Samaritan Temple is burnt, and we read in Josephus how the inhabitants of Idumaea and Ituraea were offered the alternative of circumcision or exile. It was under such circumstances that Galilee and Peraea became Jewish districts: the inhabitants were more or less forcibly converted to Judaism, but they were predominantly of Gentile blood.

On the other hand it is probable that the accounts of wholesale depopulation which we read of in ancient history are never entirely trustworthy. The people of south-eastern England are not as fair-haired and blue-eyed as they ought to be, if the Keltic aborigines had been really as completely exterminated, both men and women, as the Saxon Chronicle would have us imagine. And similarly we may believe that the Assyrian and Babylonian Captivities did not really

[1] It should be added that all our extant texts of the *Testaments*, even the Armenian version, contain Christian glosses and interpolations. See *Journal of Theological Studies* x 135-141 (Oct., 1908), where the present writer stated his reasons at length for rejecting Charles's textual theories.

mean the entire removal of the population off the soil. The great men were taken away, but the poor and landless, who were equally Israelites, remained. Gentile immigrants were afterwards introduced, and much mixture of race followed, but the main stock persisted. There was much to be said for the view that if you wanted to find the descendants of the Ten Tribes, you should look for them on the spot, that Joseph was in Samaria, Naphtali in Galilee, Reuben and Gad in Peraea. True, they have abandoned the practice of religion, but that can be remedied: let them be circumcised and keep the Law, and they will be as good Israelites as their fathers.

This last theory certainly represents the later policy of the Asmonaean princes, and the *Testaments of the Twelve Patriarchs*, the book that so warmly glorifies the Asmonaeans, seems to me to try to put that policy on a quasi-scientific and historical basis.[1] I regard it as originally addressed to these newly-made Israelites, calling them, in the name of their ancestors, to rally round Levi in the person of the priest-king, John Hyrcanus. These new subjects were not Jews, in the narrower sense of 'men of the tribe of Judah', but they might claim to be genuine representatives of the Ten Tribes.

And that is why there is so large a quantity of ethical instruction in the *Testaments*. It is because the converts needed instruction in Jewish morality as well as in Jewish patriotism and the Jewish Law. It cannot be too often repeated that we wrong the Jews, if we think of their great struggle against Hellenization as merely a blind preference for their ancestral ceremonial. The Law of the LORD was a canon of family and social life as well as a ritual system, and the pious Martyrs whose steadfastness had consecrated the revolt against Antiochus Epiphanes had laid down their lives for an ethical and social ideal quite as much as for a food law. In the 2nd century B.C., in Palestine, the two things, to us so different, were inseparable.

The hopeful anticipations with which the reign of John Hyrcanus began had clouded over before his death. It soon became evident that the Anointed of God could not be recognised in the later repre-

[1] See especially *Joseph* xix 1 ff. in the Armenian recension. Joseph says: "I saw twelve harts feeding, and nine were dispersed, but the three were preserved and the next day they also were dispersed. And I saw that the three harts were becoming three lambs, and they cried unto the Lord and the Lord brought them into a well-watered place. . . And there they cried unto the Lord until there the nine harts were gathered unto them and they became as twelve sheep. . . . . . . And ye my children, honour Levi and Judah for from them will arise the salvation of Israel." Here evidently the Tribes of Northern Israel are regarded as being in the same place as the "Jews", i. e. in Palestine.

sentatives of the Maccabean dynasty. Judas Maccabaeus and his brothers had risen to power as the leaders of the revolt against the introduction of Gentile ways of life into Israel. They actually did accomplish the restoration of the Temple worship at Jerusalem. But by no possible means could the great-nephews of Judas be regarded as the Messiah: they were worldly, tyrannical, weak. And in a couple of generations the Holy City had been taken by Pompey, and Herod—an Edomite—was on the throne, ruling over the Chosen People.

It is no wonder that in the later Apocalypses the Maccabean princes, when they are noticed at all, are regarded as a mere incident in Jewish history.[1] With the rise of Herod to power, and the outward triumph of mere state-craft and worldly diplomacy, the hopes and aspirations of religious Jews became more and more centred on a wholly miraculous intervention of God for the Redemption of Israel. Even the author of the Psalms of Solomon, a writer who hardly belongs to the circle we are considering, gives up all hope of the priest-kings. He is perhaps better acquainted with the Old Testament than with the actual state of affairs in Jerusalem, but he knows at least that nothing is to be expected from the Asmonaeans or the priestly aristocracy, and he takes refuge in the hope that somehow or other—how, he does not explain—a Prince of the House of David will appear, raised up providentially by God, in accordance with His promise recorded in Holy Writ.[2] The LORD Himself is King over Israel for ever and ever, but this Son of David may also be called "Christ the Lord".[3] 'Happy they that shall be in those days, to see the good things of Israel in the gathering of the Tribes,—may God perform it!'[4] It is a last flicker of the old prophetic conception of the Messiah as a victorious earthly ruler, a conception that does not include the new Apocalyptic doctrine of the New World.

Very different from the Psalms of Solomon, and characteristically Semitic, is the work known as the *Assumption of Moses*. There can be little doubt that this is a Palestinian document and that it was written a few years after the death of Herod the Great.[5] I fear this

[1] I mention here, by way of protest, the theory of Dr Charles, who regards "the kings and the mighty and all who possess the earth" of Enoch lxii 6 (and elsewhere in the Similitudes) as meant for the Maccabean princes: see his Note to Enoch xxxviii 5. I think the author of the Similitudes of Enoch takes a more general view of things, and that these kings and potentates represent the great Gentile Empires and World-powers: compare Rev vi 15.

[2] *Ps. Sol.* xvii 5, 23. [3] *v.* 36. [4] *v.* 50.

[5] The most probable date is A. D. 6, soon after the deposition of Archelaus. See

curious piece is not so well known as it deserves to be. No doubt this is mainly because of the unsatisfactory state of the text. The *Assumption of Moses* is extant only in a single very ancient Latin MS, a palimpsest, and very hard to decipher. The Latin text of this MS is itself full of all sorts of absurd blunders of transcription, and the lost Greek, of which the Latin is a literal translation, must have contained some serious errors, which often quite spoil the sense. And then, as in the case of Enoch, the Greek was a translation from a lost Semitic original, either Hebrew or Aramaic. It is no wonder that the meaning of whole sentences is often quite obscure, and that scholars differ seriously in their attempts to restore the original.

But the general interpretation and tendency of the work is clear enough. The "Testaments of the Twelve Patriarchs" were the last dying-speeches of the ancestors of the Tribes, the "Assumption of Moses" gives the last speech of Moses to Joshua before he is taken up Mount Pisgah to disappear from mortal eyes. As in so many other of the Apocalypses the matter takes the form of prophetical history of Israel. No names are mentioned, of course,[1] but the Captivity and the Return are clearly indicated.[2] Then follows, according to the Apocalyptist, an evil time. Those who offer the sacrifices will not be priests but "slaves, born of slaves"[3]: these are the Hellenizing priests, such as that Menelaus of whom we read in 2 Maccabees. Then will come a line of kings who will be called Priests of the Most High God, i.e. the Maccabean princes, and after them "an insolent king not of the race of the priests, a man bold and shameless, who will judge them as they deserve, for 34 years"[4]: this is obviously Herod. Next comes a reference to Varus, the Roman Governor of Syria, who suppressed a Jewish rebellion in 4 B.C., but here the history ends and the Apocalyptist looks into the future. He sees luxury and oppression on every side in high places and anticipates another visitation of wrath, when the king of the kings of the earth will crucify the faithful who confess circumcision and give their wives to the Gentiles and make their children blaspheme.[5] Then there will be a man of the tribe of Levi, whose name will be Taxo, who will take his seven sons into the wilderness to fast for three days and then die, rather than transgress the commandments of the Lord of lords;[6] thereupon the Kingdom of God will appear and Israel will be avenged. For

the article called *Moses, Assumption of*, in Hastings' Dictionary of the Bible by the present writer.

[1] See above, p. 19.
[2] *Ass. Moseos* i–iv.
[3] *Ibid.* v.
[4] *Ibid.* vi.
[5] *Ibid.* vii, viii.
[6] *Ibid.* ix.

"The Heavenly One will arise from His royal throne,
and come forth from His holy habitation, with indignation and wrath for His sons.
And earth will tremble to its utmost bounds,
and the high mountains be brought low and the forests fall,
The sun will not give light, and the horns of the moon will become dark,
they will be broken and it all will be turned into blood,
and the circle of the stars will be shattered.
The seas will sink into the abyss,
the fountains of water will fail and the rivers will be afraid,
For the Most High will arise, the Eternal God alone,
He will come in glory to do vengeance on the Gentiles and destroy all their idols.
Then happy wilt thou be, O Israel! . . ."

And so in the end God's Chosen People will be exalted to heaven, from whence they will look down in triumph upon all their enemies below.[1]

This is the climax of Moses' prophecy to Joshua. The rest of the book contains the installation of Joshua as Moses' successor, and the lost conclusion probably was occupied with the dispute between Michael and Satan over the body of Moses, referred to in the Epistle of Jude. We must not linger here over the many minor problems offered by the text.[2] What we are now concerned with is the general outlook on the future which the *Assumption of Moses* presents.

Like so many things that come down to us from the Jews, it is a strange mixture of hope and despair, of prejudice and insight. The writer has little knowledge of history or of the world beyond what he has learnt from his Bible,[3] and, like Tertullian after him, he tells us that a prominent feature of the triumph of the Elect will be the sight of their vanquished enemies. But that will be in the New Age, when everything will have changed except the personalities of men.

[1] *Ass. Moseos* x.

[2] The name *Taxo* or *Taxo*(*c*) is almost certainly derived from an artificial mis-writing of Eleazar (אלעזר = תכסוק, taking the next letter in the Semitic Alphabet): see 2 Macc vi 18 ff., and also the art. on the *Assumption* in Hastings' *D B* iii 449 above referred to, where reasons are given for accepting the traditional order of the chapters, as given in the Milan Palimpsest.

[3] That the horns of the moon could be broken appears to have shocked scholars, but Mohammed tells us that the Moon will be broken in sunder when the Hour arrives (اقتربت الساعة وانشق القمر *Qoran* liv 1). And those Manichees who thought of the New Moon as a boat must have regarded the horns as really shaped like the ends of a gondola. See also M. R. James, *Apocrypha Anecdota* II 167.

Meanwhile, in the Interim, while the sun and moon still continue, what strikes us in the expectations of the writer of the *Assumption* is the resemblance to Christian expectations as preserved in the Synoptic Gospels. The Woes on the Pharisees and Sadducees, the great Tribulation, the πειρασμόσ or trial which lies before the faithful, the hopelessness of resisting evil, the abomination of desolation in the holy place, the flight of the Saints into the wilderness,—all the Eschatology of the Gospel except the Central Figure,—it is all implied in the *Assumption of Moses*. And more than this: it is not only in the *mise-en-scène* that we find the analogy. It is in the sacred drama also. The voluntary death of the holy Taxo has a redeeming value, for it hastens the End[1]; it is effective, it acts like the death of the son of the Lord of the Vineyard in the Parable of the Wicked Husbandmen.

Thus by following the chronological order we arrive at the Apocalyptic idea as presented by the Gospels themselves. But before we leave strictly Jewish ground, we must go forward and glance at a couple of remarkable works, the two latest of the great Jewish Apocalypses, both of them written after the Destruction of Jerusalem by Titus.

The *Apocalypse of Baruch* and the book best known to English readers as *Second Esdras* are so closely related in thought and language that they have been conjectured to be the work of the same author. Some scholars, on the other hand, split up each of the two books into several documents, in which different tendencies are detected. Speaking generally, it may be said that the division of Apocalypses into their original conjectured constituents is an extremely delicate task, for it assumes that these anticipations, these dreams of the future, will be self-consistent. A certain degree of consistency we must indeed expect. The work of the same man will, to a certain extent, always breathe the same spirit. But his pictures of the future will not always harmonize in detail. Moreover, I venture to think that we must allow for the disturbing influence of real Visions, i. e. pictures seen by the writer in dream or ecstasy. There has probably been every grade of imaginative writing in this class of literature. Some of the so-called Visions in the Apocalypse of Baruch, like the dreams of Nebuchadnezzar in the canonical Daniel, read like conscious inventions: every detail in them is completely

[1] '*Hoc enim si faciemus et moriemur, sanguis noster uindicabitur coram Domino.*' *Et tunc parebit Regnum Illius* (ix 7, x 1).

and satisfactorily explained in the subjoined explanation. On the other hand, it is surely impossible to read the first chapter of the canonical Apocalypse of John and not feel that, whatever explanation we may choose to make of the Vision, something like it was really experienced by the Seer. And similarly it seems to me that some of the difficulties and incoherencies of the Eagle-Vision in Second Esdras may arise from honest reminiscence of a monstrous figure seen by the writer in a vivid dream, itself partly suggested by Dan vii 19.

So far as the Apocalypse of Baruch is concerned, I really do not see why it should be regarded as composite. Esdras, on the other hand, as read in the English Bible, does require some stripping of extraneous matter. Of the 16 chapters, the two first and two last are only found in Latin, and have no claim to be part of the original Apocalypse. The remainder, *viz.* iii–xiv of 'Second Esdras', is what we have to consider. It is no longer extant in Greek, but it survives in Latin, Syriac, Armenian, Ethiopic and Arabic translations. It is on the composition of this work, which I shall call simply 'Ezra', that scholars are divided.

Ezra starts off with a phrase that invites the application of the critical knife, for the writer describes himself as 'I Salathiel who am also Ezra'.[1] The natural inference, of course, is that the author has adapted an older Salathiel-apocalypse for a new Ezra-apocalypse. There is nothing improbable in this, for there can be little doubt that most of the Apocalypses were largely based on previously existing literary works. The mischief is, that acknowledging the existence of separate 'sources' in an ancient writer does not greatly help us to reconstruct them. Biblical scholars have talked so long about J and E and D and P for the Old Testament, and about Q for the Gospels, that it is easy to delude oneself into the idea that we are actually in possession of these venerable documents. But we do not possess them, and we cannot reconstruct them with any certainty, any more than we could reconstruct S. Mark's Gospel out of S. Matthew and S. Luke, if S. Mark's Gospel was not already in our hands to tell us how to do it. Therefore even if we assume that our Ezra is based on a lost Apocalypse of Salathiel, we cannot tell what that lost Apocalypse contained. We cannot tell how much or how little of our extant Ezra is taken from the lost Salathiel, still less can we tell what those parts of Salathiel were like which the writer of Ezra rewrote or dropped altogether. All we can do is to attempt to understand the extant work, to put ourselves into the

[1] iii 1.

attitude of the writer, whether we choose to call him an 'author' or a 'redactor'. He must have regarded his own work as a more or less satisfactory unity. We can more or less hope to realize for ourselves his point of view: the point of view of the lost sources which he may have used must remain for us a matter of conjecture.

For these reasons I must continue to treat Ezra as a whole. It may be that an earlier work, dating perhaps from just after the Destruction of Jerusalem by Titus, has been revised to fit the times of Hadrian. But I cannot follow Kabisch and Mr Box in considering the conjecturally restored earlier form.[1]

In any case, the main interest of *Ezra* and *Baruch* is the light that these works throw upon the state of mind of the Jews after the Destruction of Jerusalem, those who braced themselves to remain loyal to the religion of their fathers, even after the downfall of the system upon which it had seemed to be founded.

Of the two, *Baruch* is perhaps the more illuminating, just because it is more commonplace. The writer has been utterly cast down by the loss of Jerusalem, but he comes to believe that the Mighty One[2] will ultimately make the Israelites triumph in this world, and that afterwards in the world to come the righteous will be abundantly rewarded and the sinners tormented. His main interests are immediate and practical. He has a definite message for his fellow-countrymen. Let those who are left in the Holy Land stay there,[3] and let one and all, especially the exiles, hold fast by the Law, though the Temple be destroyed. 'Zion hath been taken from us, and we have nothing now save the Mighty One and His Law,[4] but 'if ye have respect unto the Law and are intent upon wisdom, the lamp will not fail and the shepherd will not depart and the fountain will not run dry'.[5] This is the last message of the great series of Jewish Apocalypses. As Daniel shews us what was the spirit that nerved the pious Ḥasīdīm to resist Antiochus, so Baruch lets us see in what frame of mind it was possible for the Rabbis under Johanan ben Zakkai and his successors to sit down and adapt the religion and the hopes of Israel to the times of the long dominion of the Gentiles.

The interest of *Ezra* is somewhat different, and lies in the personality of the writer. The fate anticipated for Israel in *Ezra* is not very unlike that in *Baruch*, but it affects the seers differently. The

[1] Especially in rejecting iv 52–v 13 a, vi 11–29, vii 26–44, viii 63–ix 12, from the 'Salathiel-apocalypse'.

[2] This is the usual title of God in *Baruch*. Ἰσχυρόσ actually occurs in the small surviving fragment of the Greek: it implies *El* in the original Semitic.

[3] *Baruch* lxxvii 6. [4] lxxxv 3. [5] lxxvii 16.

author of *Ezra* is not really a pessimist, in the sense of believing that evil is ultimately victorious in this world. The last act in the world-drama, according to him, is the glorious 400 years' reign of Messiah: then comes the other world of full retribution.[1] The scheme satisfies the Most High, Who says 'Let the multitude perish which was born in vain'.[2] The really interesting thing is that it does not satisfy *Ezra*. 'This is my first and last saying', says he, 'that it had been better that the earth had not given Adam, or else when it had given him to have restrained him from sinning.'[3] 'We are tormented, because we perish and know it. Let the race of men lament and the beasts of the field be glad, for it is better with them than with us; for they look not for judgement, neither do they know of torments or of salvation promised unto them after death.[4] There is nothing of this arraignment of Providence in *Baruch*: indeed, there is very little like it either in Jewish or in Christian literature, till we come to modern times.

[1] *Ezra* vii 28–33: "My Son the Messiah (*sic*) shall be revealed . . . and shall rejoice them that remain 400 years. And after these years My Son the Messiah shall die and all that have the breath of life, and the world shall be turned into the ancient silence seven days, like as in the first beginning, so that no man is left. And after seven days . . . the earth will give up those that sleep in it . . . and the Most High will be revealed upon the throne of judgement." The Messiah is not killed by enemies or disease; he just ceases (like the electric light when the switch is turned off) at the height of his triumphal career, and no one outlives him. Thus this world ends with the discomfiture of the ungodly, and the next world of individual retribution follows at once.

A somewhat similar idea underlies the conception of the End sketched in 1 Cor xv 24, 26, 28, where death is destroyed as the *last* enemy. S. Paul, however, has a special 'mystery' for his initiates, by which the necessity of death for the surviving Christians is avoided. The Christian Messiah, of course, will not have to die, for His death is past and He is always living in the New Age; S. Paul further instructs the Corinthians that the surviving Christians will be transubstantiated instead of dying and rising again (1 Cor xv 51).

[2] *Ezra* ix 22. [3] vii 46 [116]. [4] vii 64 ff.

IV. EARLY CHRISTIAN APOCALYPTIC WRITING.

Christian Apocalypses may be conveniently grouped in three main classes. First come those which do not differ in their general scope and tendency from the Jewish Apocalypses which we have been considering. I do not mean that it is impossible to tell whether it is a Christian or a Jew who is speaking. What I mean is that the general subject-matter is the same and the object of expectation is the same. When we hear from the Gospel the Discourse on the Mount of Olives,[1] or read the final chapter of the Didache, we are wholly within the region of Jewish apocalyptic thought. The subject is the near-approaching End of all things in this world, when the Elect of God spoken of by Daniel and by Enoch will come with the clouds of heaven. The Christians know Who the Messiah will be, but that is the only difference.

To Christian converts trained in Jewish thought and literature this was a natural way, in fact *the* natural way, to 'assert eternal Providence', but it was very far from being the natural way for the converts from the heathen world. Moreover, as the years went by and the End was not yet, the fact of dead individual Christians awaiting the End demanded ever more pressing recognition. The Gentile converts had joined the Church without having clear expectations of a common general catastrophe which was at the same time a vindication of right and truth and a punishment of wrong and error, but many of them did believe that the man of insight and virtue would gain a happy immortality when he was freed at death from the burden of the flesh. In direct accordance with these ideas there sprang up at least as early as the end of the first Christian century a new apocalyptic, dealing not with the Last Judgement, but with the fate of individual souls and individual courses of conduct. So far as we know, this second series of Christian Apocalypses begins with the *Apocalypse of Peter*, happily rediscovered about a quarter of a century ago. The Apocalypse of Peter, in its original form, was condemned as heretical, but it survived in countless imitations and adaptations, and at last was set forth on the grandest scale in Dante's

[1] Mk xiii and parallels.

Divine Comedy. The general scheme is of the very simplest; the dead souls are taken one by one to the place they deserve and an attempt is made, more or less, to 'make the punishment fit the crime'. As I pointed out at the very beginning of these Lectures, this is a fundamentally different idea from that of the Last Judgement and of the genuine Jewish Apocalypses, which are animated by the idea of the impending catastrophe that is going to usher in a New Age for all the world.

But besides the Jewish Apocalypse and the Pagan Apocalypse there is a third form of Christian Apocalypse, worth some attention, not so much for its intrinsic value as for the way in which it illustrates the profound difference which really, though to some extent unconsciously, separated the Christian view of history from the Jewish. The ancient Christian work called the *Ascension of Isaiah* is the best illustration of this third type of Apocalypse, which while Jewish in form is essentially Christian in its outlook.

The *Ascension of Isaiah* in its general plan recalls the Book of Daniel. Of the eleven chapters into which the book is now divided, chaps. vi–xi give the vision of Isaiah when he was transported into the seventh heaven and witnessed the Descent of the Beloved (i.e. the Heavenly Christ, the Son of God), through the seven heavens down to earth, followed by His victorious return. The earlier chapters, which also contain the account of a vision, give a historical setting to the vision at the end. They tell us how Isaiah saw the vision in the days of Hezekiah and how he was sawn in sunder with a wooden saw by Manasseh, Hezekiah's wicked son, who was instigated to do the deed by Beliar, i.e. the evil spirit who dwells in man and the adversary of everything to do with Christ.[1]

I sometimes fancy that the spirit of Beliar must be dwelling in some of my friends when they use the wooden saw to dissect the *Ascension of Isaiah*. Notwithstanding their efforts it continues to the end to speak with a Christian voice, just as Isaiah did.[2] I shall venture here to treat it as a unity and as the work of a Christian throughout. Of course, I do not mean to deny that some details in the fanciful story of Isaiah's martyrdom may have been ultimately derived from Jewish sources. But that is a very different thing from regarding the narrative portions of the *Ascension of Isaiah* as a Jewish document which can be detached from the rest of the work and represented as an independent whole. On the contrary, I regard it as an integral part of the *Ascension*, constructed from the writer's

[1] S. Paul uses the name Beliar in a similar way, 2 Cor vi 15.

[2] See *Asc. Isai.* v 14 f.

knowledge of the early imperfect Greek translation of the Books of Kings, supplemented here and there by stray fragments of Jewish lore.[1]

The interest of the *Ascension of Isaiah* lies in its early date. In the earlier apocalyptic section we find that Beliar is expected to "descend from his firmament in the likeness of a man, a lawless king, the slayer of his mother".[2] This is obviously a reference to Nero. It is true that the Antichrist here announced is Beliar in the likeness of Nero, not Nero himself. But it appears that Nero is the only persecuting Emperor known to the apocalyptist, and in any case I do not believe that the Nero-myth was a creative force after the first third of the 2nd century. Descriptions of Antichrist modelled on the belief in *Nero redivivus* persisted for centuries, but I do not imagine that they were newly made after about 130 or 140 A. D.

This would give the early part of the 2nd century as the date of the Nero passage in the *Ascension of Isaiah*, and it seems to me that the rest of the work cannot be later. The only exception is xi 2–22 of the Ethiopic text, a passage which excites suspicion by naming Joseph and Mary, against the usual rule that apocalyptic prophecies are silent about names. At this point a Slavonic and a Latin text of the *Ascension* are extant, and they omit most of the passage,[3] so that we may safely conclude either that the Ethiopic is here interpolated, or that the original form of the passage was quite different.

With all respect to the great scholars who have worked at the *Ascension of Isaiah*, I cannot but think that the author of the work is more skilful than they take him to be, and that the unsatisfactory impression which it makes as a whole is due more to the nature of the task which the writer set before him than to the manner in which he has carried it out. It is the old mistake, which has spoilt so many clever works of art, the mistake of trying to do two things at once, of trying to serve two masters.

In this case the two masters are the Last Judgement and the Incarnation.

The emotional effect of apocalyptic writing, as exhibited in the great series which extends from the Book of Daniel to the Apocalypse of Baruch, is that everything is subordinated to the announcement

[1] See Appendix II.

[2] *Asc. Isai.* iv 2. The Greek contains the rare word μητραλῴασ : where else in Christian literature does it occur? The writer of the *Ascension* uses one or two words not very common in ecclesiastical Greek, such as ἐξαφιέναι, 'to desert or neglect.' And has not the epithet of Beliar, which the Ethiopic version renders Maṭanbūchūs (ii 4) or *Mechēmbēchūs* (v 3), something to do with *metempsychosis*? See further, p. 74.

[3] Including all mention of Joseph and Mary.

of the End. Everything leads up to the Judgement and to the New Age that follows it. It is because the End is so often forgotten in the *Testaments of the XII Patriarchs* that parts of them are so wearisome to read. But in the *Ascension of Isaiah* the idea that the End is the chief thing in history is crossed by the new Christian idea that it is the Incarnation of the Messiah, an event now passed, which is the chief thing in history. This new Christian idea, that began with S. Paul and attained more and more fixity and definiteness as time went on, is really fatal to great apocalyptic writing. The Incarnation, the career of Jesus Christ, may be the most important fact in all history past or future; but if so, an Apocalypse is not the proper literary form in which to set it forth. When the older Apocalyptists, as in the *Book of Enoch* or the *Assumption of Moses*, sketch the past history of Israel, it always leads up to the future history as anticipated by the Seer.

The work of the Apocalyptists belongs to the sphere of Hope: the vision of Isaiah, when stripped of its apocalyptic machinery, belongs to the sphere of 'the Faith' in its technical theological sense. It is really a piece of 'dogmatics', an essay in Christology. But when we once recognise this, I think we ought to admire the skill with which the writer of the *Ascension of Isaiah* has poured his new wine into the old bottles. It is an Apocalypse, so he must tell us about the End: on the other hand, his real interest is in his theological doctrine about the Descent of the Christ through the seven heavens, how it came about that He was not observed, and how He victoriously ascended and sat down on the right hand of the Great Glory. So our Apocalyptist contrives to bring in the part about the End in a kind of parenthesis: Isaiah is arrested by Manasseh at the instigation of Beliar, "for Beliar was in great wrath against Isaiah . . . because through him the going forth of the Beloved had been made known, and His transformation . . . and that He should be crucified . . . and afterwards His disciples will forsake the teaching,"[1] . . . and so it drops into *oratio recta* and direct prediction. At the end of the predictions the writer resumes his story by saying "On account of these visions, therefore, Beliar was wroth with Isaiah, and he dwelt in the heart of Manasseh, and he sawed Isaiah in sunder with a wooden saw".[2] Then follows the story of the actual martyrdom.

This ingenious anticipation of the Vision of Isaiah leaves the writer free to leave out all about the End, when he comes to the Vision itself, which concludes impressively with the Heavenly Session of the victorious Christ. I cannot help feeling that it is very cleverly

[1] *Asc. Isai.* iii 13 ff. [2] *Ibid.* v 1.

done. Of course there are inconsistencies, which learned persons detect, who read the book as it was never intended to be read. But on the whole the *Ascension of Isaiah* gives me the impression of a literary unity, and the inconsistencies seem to me to be due rather to the divided aim of the author than to the mechanical combination of separable documents.

The Apocalypses have surely had rather hard measure dealt out to them during the last fifty years. They were written for a very different kind of public from the learned persons who study them now so conscientiously. Now they are hardly read save by trained scholars, men trained in the use of ancient historical documents, who moreover have no illusions as to the historical value of the 'revelations' which the Apocalypses profess to contain. They study them to learn the ideas and prejudices, the hopes and fears, of their writers. It is all done by the most scientific methods, and the chief danger now is that too strict a standard of consistency and rationality may be exacted from writers to whom consistency and rationality were quite secondary considerations. Consistency and rationality belong to the past, and to the course of events in this world: the Apocalyptist's part is to stimulate his comrades by sketches of the future. And a future in which everything is consistent and in which, nevertheless, universal justice is done is a Vision which the heart of man has not conceived.

Think for a moment of some patent inconsistencies to be found in the Apocalypse of S. John. In what state does the Seer see the souls of them who had been slain for the word of God? Are they not underneath the Altar, crying out 'How long, O Lord?' And they are told to rest yet a little longer, till the number of the martyrs is made up.[1] They also, like the Lamb that had been slain, are a sacrifice, and they are impatient for the long-delayed consummation. But then who are the great multitude that no man could number, who come from the great tribulation and have made their robes white in the blood of the Lamb, who for that very reason are now before the throne of God?[2] Are these better off than the Martyrs? Both visions belong to *this* time, the time before the End. And again, how does the picture of the impatient Martyrs harmonize with 'Blessed are the dead which die in the Lord from henceforth, for they rest'?[3]

These inconsistencies are in a sense real, and I am quite ready to

[1] Rev vi 9–11: that this is no isolated figure, taken mechanically from earlier documents, appears from xvi 7, where the Altar voices the ultimate satisfaction of the slain souls.

[2] Rev vii 9–17.

[3] Rev xiv 13.

believe that the ultimate cause of them is a mingling of different and inconsistent sources. There is the authentic Jewish source which defers the Judgement and the great Adjustment of all things to the fast-approaching End; there is the Pagan sentiment that the Adjustment, if it take place at all, must take place at once after the death of each individual; and there is the specifically Christian belief that somehow the Coming of Jesus Christ has made all the difference, and that the New Age must date from His Passion and Resurrection, even if that be patently not the Harvest but merely an early Paschal sheaf of firstfruits.

But these three distinct ideas exist simultaneously in the mind of the Christian Apocalyptist. It is not a question of the fitting together of documents, of scissors and paste, but of the alternate emergence of independent convictions into consciousness and expression. In moments of crisis and emotion these convictions sometimes attain an artistic unity, held together by a feeling of passionate and unshaken loyalty to God and His Christ, but they do not attain, and cannot attain, to logical consistency.

After all, a logical Apocalypse would most likely be a dull Apocalypse. And unless the point of view which I have put before you in these Lectures is altogether mistaken, the impulse which produced the great Apocalypses was not a logical theory, but a passionate conviction, roused to utterance by the events of Jewish history. The doctrine of the Apocalypses is the doctrine of the approaching Judgement, and the doctrine of the approaching Judgement was in essence an expression of the Jews' unquenchable conviction that God would not altogether allow His Chosen People to perish in their struggle with the Civilization of the heathen world.

The Apocalyptic literature is thus the product of one particular set of historical conditions. In accordance with this, real historical events which can be identified are often referred to or indicated, and such indications where they are certain are most valuable for giving us the date of particular passages or even of whole works. But it is possible to press some of the details too closely, to look for references to contemporary history in passages where the Apocalyptist's points of view were more vague and general, or more frankly supernatural. I do not think we find the squabbles of Jewish factions reflected in the Judgement-scene of the *Similitudes* of Enoch; I do not think there is any prophecy of the siege of Jerusalem by Titus in the Discourse on the Mount of Olives as given in S. Mark. It is true that the apocalyptic Hope was evoked by the pressure of contemporary struggles and took its classical shape from books that directly reflect those struggles. But when the political crisis had passed, the Hope remained. The actual resistance, active and passive, of the Jewish nation to the Hellenizing efforts of Antiochus revealed both to Jews and to Gentiles that in Judaism there was an element incompatible with the rest of the then civilized world: some New Thing, some New state of things, must come to pass, if Israel was to rest satisfied.

The new state of things did come to pass, different as it was from what the apocalyptist Seers had looked for, and two distinct Societies grew up, each claiming to be the true Israel to whom the promises had been given. Of these, it was the new congregation of the Gentiles, and not Israel after the flesh, which continued to cherish the Apocalypses, until the day came that their message was obviously antiquated and they were laid aside and forgotten. Now that some of the spirit of life has come again into the scattered bones of this literature, and they have come up out of their graves and have been brought into their own land again, we moderns, both of the Church and of the Synagogue, may be grateful to the Early Christians for preserving them.

APPENDICES

APPENDIX I.

ON THE GREEK TEXT OF ENOCH.

THE primary object of this Note is to give some justification for the general approval of the text of the Gizeh MS (G), now at Cairo, as compared with the Ethiopic (E) and the extracts in Georgius the Syncellus (S), expressed in Lecture II, pp. 26, 27.

1. *The Descent of the Angels* (Enoch vi 1–6).

I give a translation of the text of G, with the variants of E and S.

1. And it came to pass when the sons of men were multiplied, in those days there were born daughters beautiful and fair. 2. And the Angels, sons of Heaven, saw them and desired them, and said to one another 'Come, let us choose for ourselves wives from men and beget for ourselves children'. 3. And Semiazas said to them, he who was their leader, 'I fear lest ye will not be willing to do this deed and I shall be alone guilty of a great sin'. 4. So they all answered him 'We will swear all of us with an oath and bind one another with a curse not to frustrate this plan until we accomplish it and do this deed'. 5. Then they all sware together and bound each other with a curse in it. 6. . . . .

1 in those days] *om.* S born] + to them ES and fair] *om.* S 2 *init.* And the Watchers desired them and went astray after them and said S Come] *om.* S men] + of the earth S and beget . . . children] *om.* S 3 he who was] *om.* S 4 So (οὖν)] And ES answered him] + and said S (*and some* MSS E) and do this deed] *om.* S: *for* until . . . deed E *has* 'and we will do for this plan the deed 6. See below.

It will be seen that in vi 1–5 the variants are trifling, but the Syncellus habitually abridges redundant expressions, while in *ver.* 2 he frankly paraphrases. This is exactly what one expects in a man quoting a work which he does not regard as textually authoritative, and it should make us very wary of regarding variations attested by the Syncellus alone as resting on anything else than his own free alterations.

For *ver.* 6 we are most unluckily deprived of G, the scribe's pen having wandered from καὶ ἀνεθεμάτισαν ἀλλήλουσ ἐν αὐτῷ to the corresponding words in *ver.* 6. S has

> ἦσαν δὲ οὗτοι διακόσιοι οἱ καταβάντεσ ἐν ταῖσ ἡμέραισ Ἰάρεδ εἰσ τὴν κορυφὴν τοῦ Ἑρμονιεὶμ ὄρουσ καὶ ἐκάλεσαν τὸ ὄροσ Ἑρμώμ, καθότι ὤμοσαν καὶ ἀνεθεμάτισαν ἀλλήλουσ ἐν αὐτῷ.

The literal translation of E is

> And they in all were two hundred, and they came down upon Ardīs which is the top of Mount Armēn, and they called the mountain Armen, because they sware in it and bound each other with a curse.

Dr Charles accepts S as substantially genuine and regards E as corrupt. He further accepts Halévi's conjecture that there was in the original text not only a play upon the name of Hermon, but also upon the name of Jared. Jared (יֶרֶד) seems to mean 'Descent', from the Hebrew word for 'to descend': the word does not occur in Aramaic, so that on this view the passage was originally written in Hebrew.

Our first business is to retranslate the Ethiopic into the underlying Greek. This is fairly easy. *Armen* is the standing equivalent for 'Hermon' (or 'Hermonim'). For the decisive clause we thus get

οἱ κατέβησαν ΕΠΙΑΡΔΕΙϹΚΟΡΥΦΗΝ τοῦ Ἑ. ὄρουσ.

A glance at S shews us that the *-is* of *Ardīs* is the preposition εἰσ, required before κορυφήν. We have therefore ΕΠΙΑΡΔ corresponding to ἐν ταῖσ ἡμέραισ Ἰάρεδ in S. I venture to suggest that these four words are nothing more than an ingenious paraphrase made by the Syncellus himself.

That it is wrong I judge for the following reasons: (1) the Ethiopic has nothing corresponding to ἐν ταῖσ ἡμέραισ except the preposition ἐπί. It is most unlikely, even if grammatically just possible, that the original Greek translation of Enoch would have expressed 'in Jared's time' by ἐπὶ Ἰάρεδ (or ἐπ' Ἰάρ[ε]δ), without any note of office or qualification. (2) The proper place for specifying the time of the descent of the Sons of God is not here but in vi 1. In that verse it is vaguely described as 'in those days' by G and E, but this note of time is left out by S, obviously because in *ver.* 6 he was going to date it precisely. (3) The argument that there is in *Enoch* a play upon the name 'Jared' and the verb 'to descend' is a modern conjecture: the play upon the 'curse' (*ḥerm*) and the name 'Hermon', on the other hand, is definitely pointed out in the text itself.

Further, I think we can guess that the actual source from whence the Syncellus derived his conjecture was the Book of Jubilees, a work elsewhere expressly quoted by him. In *Jub.* iv 15 the birth of Jared is mentioned: "and he [Mahaleel] called his name Jared; for in his days the angels of the Lord descended on the earth, those named the Watchers." Here no doubt we have a Hebrew original and a play on the words *yārĕdu* and *Yárĕd.* But it has nothing to do with the Book of Enoch, and when in *Jub.* v the actual story of the descent of the Angels is told, perhaps from the passage in Enoch, the name of Jared is never mentioned.[1]

But what, then, are we to make of ΕΠΙΑΡΔ in Enoch vi 6, if it has nothing to do with the Patriarch Jared? I venture to suggest that the original Greek translation had ΕΠΙΑΡΑ, *i.e.* ἐπὶ ἄρα, and that ἄρα was supposed by the translator to be the name of the summit of Hermon. The original Aramaic would be

ונחתו לארע לריש טורא דחרמון

'And they came down below to the top of Mount Hermon.' לְאֲרַע, also written לְרַע, means 'lower'. In Targ J~II~ to Gen xl 23 דלרע is used for 'belonging to here below' (*d'ici-bas*), but what is meant in Enoch may be 'on Hermon, below the clouds and the snow-line'. If this conjecture be adopted, and it involves only reading Δ for Α in the Greek text implied by the Ethiopic, we get a text free from every difficulty. But it definitely implies an Aramaic basis, not a Hebrew one.

This is probably the most convenient point to record my opinion that the mention of the three diverse races of monsters in Syncellus's paraphrase of Enoch vii, *viz.* Giants, Naphilim and Elioud,[2] does not go back to the true text of Enoch, but is derived directly from Jubilees vii 22. If the Naphilim are anywhere mentioned in Enoch, it is in xv 11, where G (and E) have ΝΕΦΕΛΑΣ: so Bouriant and Flemming.

2. *The Prologue to Enoch.*

The Prologue to the Book of Enoch, i. e. Enoch i–v, seems to me to deserve a special study, especially with regard to the style of the author and the methods of the translator of the Ethiopic version. Except for some Patristic quotations in i 9 the only extant authorities here are the Cairo MS (G) and the Ethiopic (E). I give a literal translation of each in parallel columns. Words and sentences found only in G but not in E (and *vice versa*) are printed in italics.

[1] The Appendix *On the Birth of Noah*, which is added to the Ethiopic text of Enoch (chap. cvi–cviii), also states that the Angels transgressed in the days of Jared (spelt *Īyārēṯ*). But this Appendix has no real literary connexion with the genuine Enoch, which ends with the 'Amen' of cv 2.

[2] Here again we have a confusion of *d* and *a*, for the Ethiopic of *Jub.* vii 22 has *Elyo*, probably corresponding to ΕΛΙΟΥΑ.

Enoch — Greek

I 1 The word of the blessing of Enoch, how he blessed elect righteous men,
who will be there in the day of distress for taking away all the
adversaries and righteous men *shall be saved.*

2 And he took up his parable and said :
Enoch, a righteous man *is he,*
a vision from God for him was opened †having†,
the vision of the Holy One and of heaven He shewed me,
and holy apologues[1] I myself heard,
and *as* I heard from them all things and I myself knew
as I looked.
And not for the present generation *did I consider,*
but for one far distant *do I speak*;
3 and concerning the elect I *now* say it,
and concerning them have I taken up *my* parable.
And *my* Holy One, the Great One, will come forth from His habitation,
4 *and* the God of eternity upon the earth will tread on Mount Sinai,
and will appear from His encampment,
and will appear in the power of His might from the heaven *of*
heavens.
5 And all will fear, and the Watchers will †believe†,
and †*they will sing*† *secret things in all the ends of the* [*earth*],
and all the ends of the earth will be shaken,
and trembling and great fear will take hold of them unto the
uttermost parts of the earth.
6 And high mountains will shake *and fall and dissolve,*
and high hills will be laid low, *that mountains should waste away,*
and they will melt like wax in front *of the fire* in flame.
7 And the earth will be torn *into pieces by a rent,*
and all things that are on the earth will be destroyed.
And there will be a judgement on all things and
8 with the righteous He will make peace,
and upon the elect there will be protection *and peace,*
and upon them shall be mercy,
and they will all belong to God and He will give them prosperity,[2]
and He will bless them *all and protect them all and help us,*
and light will shine for them,
and He will make peace upon them.
9 For He comes with His ten thousands and His holy ones
to do judgement on all,
and will destroy all the ungodly,

[1] Read ΑΠΟΛΟΓΩΝ not ΑΓΙΟΛΟΓΩΝ : the MS might be either.

[2] prosperity (= *εὐοδίαν*)] good-pleasure G (*εὐδοκίαν*) : so Charles.

Enoch — Ethiopic

I 1 The word of the blessing of Enoch, how he blessed elect and
righteous men who will be there in the day of distress for the
taking away of all the adversaries and ungodly.

2 And he answered further and said:
Enoch, a righteous man,
who from the Lord while his eyes were open, and he was seeing
the vision of the Holy One in heaven which the angels shewed me,

and I heard from them all things, and I myself understood
what I was seeing.
And not for this generation,
but for one far distant that will come,
3 concerning the elect I said it,
and I answered concerning them a parable.
The Holy and Great One will come forth from His habitation,
4 the God of eternity, and from thence he will tread upon Mount Sinai,
and will appear in His encampment,
and will appear in the power of His might from heaven.

5 And all will fear, and the Watchers will quake,

and fear and great trembling will take hold of them unto the
uttermost parts of the earth.
6 And high mountains will tremble,
and high hills will be laid low,
and they will melt like wax from the flame.
7 And the earth will be rent,
and all things that are on the earth will be destroyed.
And there will be a judgement on all things and *on all the righteous*:
8 with the righteous He will make peace,
and He will protect the elect,
and there shall be mercy upon them,
and they will all belong to God and they will prosper,[1]
and they will be blessed,
and *God's* light will shine for them.

9 And lo, He came with ten thousands of holy Ones,
to do judgement on them,
and to destroy the ungodly,

[1] Comp. *Jubilees* xxvii 16 and the Hebrew *hiṣlīḥ*.

Enoch — Greek

and will convict all flesh about all their works *of ungodliness*
which they have ungodly done,
and of all the stubborn words they have spoken,
and about all the things that ungodly sinners *have uttered*
against Him.

II 1 Observe all the things in heaven, how they do not change
their ways,
and the luminaries in heaven, how they all rise and set,
each one ordered in its *appointed* time,
and in their feasts they appear,
and they do not transgress their *own* order.
2 See the earth and consider about the things that come to pass in it
from the beginning to the end,
[*things which*] *are corruptible,*
how they change not, *no, nothing upon earth,*
but all things appear to you *as* works of God.
3 See the summer and the winter ;

III examine and see all the trees,
how

(IV)

V 1 the leaves are green in them, covering the trees,
and *all their* fruit is *for honour and glory.*
Consider *and know* about all *His works,*
and perceive that *a Living God* has made them thus,
and He lives for ever and ever.
2 And *all* His works that He has done for ever from year to year
all come to pass thus,
and all things that the works accomplish for Him,
and they do not change *their works,*
but as it were by command all things come to pass.
3 See how the sea and the rivers similarly accomplish their task,
and they change not their works *from His words.*

Enoch — Ethiopic

and to convict all flesh about all that they have done
and †prepared†[1]

the ungodly and sinners
against Him.

II 1 Observe all the things in heaven, how they do not change
their ways,
the luminaries in heaven, how they all rise and set,
each one ordered in its time,

and they do not transgress their order.
2 See the earth and consider about the things that are done in it
from the beginning to the end,

how there changes not
any work of God as it appears.
3 See the summer and the winter,
how all the earth is filled with water,
and clouds and dew and rain rest upon it.
III Observe and see all the trees,
how *they appear to be withered and all their leaves to be fallen,*
except 14 trees which do not let them fall but keep some
of the old until the new comes, for two or three years.
IV *And again, observe the days of summer, how the sun has*
been over it in its beginning, and ye seek shade and
shelter because of the heat of the sun and the earth also
burns with the warmth of the glow, and ye cannot tread the
earth or a rock because of the heat.
V 1 *Observe how* the trees with greenness of leaves cover themselves
and bear fruit.
And consider about all
and perceive that †ye have made† all of them
Who lives for ever
2 And His works before Him each year
that shall be
and all His works serve Him
and change not,
but as God commanded so all things come to pass.
3 See how the seas and the rivers similarly accomplish
their work.

[1] prepared] apparently altered from 'ungodly done' by the change of one letter so Charles.

Enoch — Greek

4 But ye, ye have not continued nor done according to His
commandments,
but have turned away and uttered great and stubborn words
with your unclean mouth against His majesty;
because ye have uttered (thus) in your lies,
O hard of heart, there will be no peace for you!
5 Therefore your days ye shall curse,
and the years of your life shall be destroyed,
and *the years of your destruction* shall be multiplied with
an eternal curse,
and there will not be for you mercy *and peace*!
6 Then will your names be for an eternal curse to all the righteous,
and by you shall curse *all they that curse,*
and all the sinners and ungodly shall swear by you.
And all the innocent[1] *will rejoice, and there will be for them*
forgiveness of sins and every mercy and peace and gentleness.
there will be for them salvation, good light,
and they will inherit the earth;
and for all you sinners there will come no salvation,
but on all of you there will lodge[2] *a curse.*
7 And for the elect there will be light and joy and peace,
and they will inherit the earth,
but for you ungodly there will be a curse.
8 Then will be given to the elect *light and grace,*
and they will inherit the earth;
then will be given to all the elect wisdom,
and they will all live,
and they will not sin any more,
neither by ignorance[3] nor by presumption,
and there will be light in an enlightened man
and in an intelligent man understanding,
9 and they will incur no guilt,
neither will they sin all the days of their life,
nor will they die by the anger of wrath,
but the number of the days of their life they will fulfil,
and their life will be lengthened in peace,
and the years of their joy will be multiplied
in gladness and peace eternal
in all the days of their life.

[1] Read *ἀναμάρτητοι* (with Swete)] G appears to have ΑΜΑΡΤΗ|ΤΟΙ but the letters ΤΗ are very faint, like some others at the end of lines on this page.

[2] Read *καταλύσει κατάρα* (so Radermacher and Charles)] ΚΑΤΑΛΥCΙΝ ΚΑΤΆΡΑΝ G.

[3] ΚΑΤΑΛΗΘΕΙΑΝ G: see the Note below.

Enoch — Ethiopic

4 But ye, ye have not continued nor done the Lord's
commandments,
but have transgressed and uttered great and stubborn words
with your unclean mouth against His majesty;

O hard of heart, there will be no peace for you!
5 And therefore your days ye shall curse,
and the years of your life shall ye destroy,
and it shall be multiplied with
an eternal curse,
and there will not be for you mercy! [righteous,
6 And in those days ye will give your name for an eternal curse to all the
and you they shall curse
the sinners †always to you together with† the sinners.

7 And for the elect there will be light and joy and peace,
and they will inherit the earth,
but for you ungodly there will be a curse.
8 And then will be given to the elect

wisdom,
and they will all live,
and they will not sin any more,
neither by ungodliness nor by presumption,
but they in whom is wisdom will humbly worship,

9 and they will not sin any more,
neither will they be condemned all the days of their life,
nor will they die by anger nor by wrath,
but the number of the days of their life they will fulfil,
and their life will be lengthened in peace,
and the years of their joy will be multiplied
in gladness and in peace eternal
in all the days of their life.

Before considering the above passage in detail some general remarks upon method may not be out of place. I have printed the Prologue in full in an intentionally quite literal English rendering, in order that my readers may gather some idea of the general condition of the extant Greek text of Enoch and of the Ethiopic version of the Greek. It is evident at the first glance that neither the Cairo text nor the Ethiopic has any pretensions to literary excellence. This was not so evident in the passage from Enoch vi, a piece of plain prose. The Prologue is more ambitious and more poetical in style and demanded greater skill in the translator.

It is, of course, highly probable that the original Aramaic or Hebrew text was a better composition than the Greek translation: it may not have had the literary merits of Amos or Isaiah, but it was probably idiomatic and forcible. The analogy of Amos and Isaiah, in fact, shews us what our position is; it is as if we had to understand and reconstruct the Prophets from the Septuagint alone. But after all it is not quite certain that the original author of the Prologue was a great stylist. In Dr Hort's words (*Introd. to N. T.*, § 27): 'There is much literature, ancient no less than modern, in which it is needful to remember that authors are not always grammatical, or clear, or consistent, or felicitous; so that not seldom an ordinary reader finds it easy to replace a feeble or half-appropriate word or phrase by an effective substitute; and thus the best words to express an author's meaning need not in all cases be those which he actually employed.' The passage now before us seems to me to fall under this condemnation, at least so far as 'vain repetitions' are concerned. Here, as elsewhere in Enoch, especially xciv–civ (a section that seems to me certainly written by the writer of the Prologue), the author thinks he will be heard for his much speaking. Such passages read like a shorthand report of an extempore sermon; the same thing is said over and over again without real difference of meaning.

The critical emendation of the text of such works is a very delicate matter, if the aim be to reproduce the original, because the more forcible reading is not always the more ancient. The main rule is that in rhetorical passages like this no wholly new idea is only expressed once; what cannot be paralleled either in the immediate context or elsewhere in the book is likely to be an interpolation, while on the other hand genuine clauses which only repeat what has been said before with slight verbal changes are liable to be dropped as superfluous, especially by impatient translators.

To come now to details, I wish to give some reason for suggesting that in the Prologue to Enoch the *plus* of the Greek is mostly genuine, but the *plus* of the Ethiopic is mostly interpolation. This is exactly the opposite of what Dr Charles and most other scholars think, so that some further explanation is needed.

The *plus* of the Ethiopic is practically confined to a single passage containing the description of summer and winter (ii 3—v 1).[1] Dr Charles says that G, which only has 'See the summer and the winter; examine and see all the trees, how the leaves are green in them covering the trees, and all their fruit is for honour and glory', has lost the rest through homoeoteleuton. But a glance at the passages as I have printed them above will shew that this cannot be the explanation. It will not explain the absence of ii $3^{b\,c}$. Further, there is in the Ethiopic text of this passage a scientific clearness and absence of rhetoric which seems to me not to accord with the rest. The sinners are bidden to consider the regularity of summer and winter: why should they turn aside to consider the (exceptional) phenomena of evergreen trees? And this in a Prologue! More probably G has preserved the original text, and the additions in E are a botanical gloss by a learned editor. As Charles points out, fourteen evergreen trees were reckoned by the Greeks (*Geoponica* xi 1), which seems to indicate that the gloss did not originate in the Ethiopic.

In i 7 the words 'on all the righteous', found in E but not in G, seem to me genuine. They might easily be omitted by a careless scribe, and they make good sense, for the 'judgement' is as much the vindication of the righteous as the punishment of the sinners.

The *plus* of the Greek is no doubt mostly needless repetition or (as in i 5^{b}) corrupt; yet, as we are not dealing with an original but a translation, it seems to me somewhat difficult to dismiss these additions as scribal blunders. The five extra clauses of G, for instance, in v 6 look very like an alternative (and more paraphrastic) translation of the three clauses of v 7, but to say this raises more difficulties than it solves. In codices of the Septuagint 'doublets' are often found side by side; but for that there is a historical cause, *viz.* the influence of Origen's *Hexapla*. In the case of Enoch we have no Origen and no *Hexapla*, and to assume the existence of variant independent readings of the original Semitic text, whether in G or E or the Syncellus, as Dr Charles sometimes does,[2] is to assume the existence of doors of access to Semitic literature on

[1] It must be remembered that the chapters were made by Dillmann before G was discovered.

[2] See e. g. Charles's notes to the Greek text on Enoch i 6^{c}, 7^{a}, $9^{c\beta}$; v 6, 8, vi 4^{b}, x 7, xiii 1, xvii 7, xxv 6, xxvii 2.

the part of Greek-speaking Christians, for which we have no warrant in general history. And if it be replied, that not Christians but Greek-speaking Jews were the correctors, then we should have to assume the preservation in Christian circles of more than one line of Enoch-codices,—in this case, the Cairo text which has the doublets and the Ethiopic text which has escaped them.

If v 6^b be regarded as a doublet to v 7 I can only suppose that v 6^b is the rough original and v 7 a literary improvement of it, the rough original having somehow in G escaped deletion. But if so, G must be regarded as preserving traces of an older form of text, of which E is a literary revision.

The moral I draw is that the transmitted text of Enoch is too bad to be thoroughly emended. Methodical exegesis of such a text is like art-criticism on the Monna Lisa based upon reproductions in the half-penny press. Such reproductions are quite good so far as they go—in some ways they give a truer impression than a carefully 'faked' engraving, but they cannot be used for minute details, and the more you look at them under the microscope the greater is the chance of misinterpretation.

The following Notes, the result of 'microscopical' study of the Prologue, are offered as suggestions, with a full acknowledgement of the small degree of certainty attainable.

i 2 is very confused, but *τὴν ὅρασιν τοῦ ἁγίου* surely goes with *ἔδειξέν μοι*. The preceding words ΗΝΕΧΩΝ I cannot translate, and *ὅρασισ ἀνεῳγμένη* is, so far as I can make out, a unique combination: 'Visions' are not 'opened', but 'seen'. In the next clause we ought perhaps to read *ἀπὸ λόγων*, not *ἀπολόγων*, as 'apologues' seem hardly ever to be mentioned in Jewish or Christian literature.

There is also a difficulty as to where Enoch's own words are supposed to begin, whether at Ἐνώχ, or at *ἄνθρωποσ*, or at *τὴν ὅρασιν*. The analogies of Balaam and of Job, who also 'take up their parable', help us very little to emend the text of G. It seems to me that if Enoch begins in the 3rd person, then his words must begin with his own name.

i 5. The *plus* of G is here so odd that it must be genuine, but both *πιστεύσουσιν* and ΚΑΙΑΣΩΣΙΝ seem to be corrupt. The *ἀπόκρυφα* must be 'hiding-places': cf. Enoch c 4

"The angels shall descend into the secret places
"And gather together into one place all those who brought down sin,

"And the Most High will arise on that Day of judgement
"To execute great judgement amongst sinners."

ii 2 *εἴσιν φθαρτά.* Swete prefixes *ὥσ*, or we might read *ἅ εἴσιν φθαρτά.* The sense must surely have been 'though they be corruptible (yet do they not change)'.

v 8 *οὐ κατ' ἀλήθειαν οὔτε κατὰ ὑπερηφανίαν.* So G. Charles reads *κατ' ἀσέβειαν* with E, but this makes no contrast to *ὑπερηφανίαν.* Surely we must read *κατ' ἄγνοιαν.*

The phrase *οὐ κατὰ . . . . . οὔτε κατὰ ὑπερηφανίαν* almost necessarily suggests the contrast of sins of presumption with those of accident, as in Ps xix (xviii) 13, 14, where both *ἄγνοια* and *ὑπερηφανία* occur together in Aquila's version: see also Lev xxii 14 (Heb. and LXX). The Aramaic phrase is לא בשלו ולא בזדנו (*lā bshālū wlā bizdānū*).

Between ΚΑΤΑΓΝΟΙΑΝ and ΚΑΤΑΛΗΘΕΙΑΝ there is not much difference (Γ = Λ, Ν = Η, Ο = Θ, Ι = ΕΙ).

3. *Enoch and the Valleys of the Dead* (*chap.* xxii).[1]

'And from thence I journeyed to another place, and he shewed me towards the West another great and high mountain of hard rock, 2 and there were four places in it, hollow, deep, and very smooth, three of them dark, and one light with a fountain of water in the midst of it.[2] And I said 'How smooth these hollows are, and deep and dark to look at!' 3 Then answered Raphael, the one of the holy angels that was with me, and said to me 'These hollow places are for gathering together the spirits of the souls[3] of the dead. For this very purpose have they been assigned,[4] that here should be gathered together all the souls of men, 4 and these places for containing them, they have been made[5] until the day of their judgement and until the

[1] See Lecture II, p. 20.

[2] Punctuate thus, i. e. *σκοτεινοί, καὶ εἶσ φωτεινὸσ καὶ πηγὴ ὕδατοσ ἀνὰ μέσον αὐτοῦ.*

[3] Throughout Enoch the 'soul' (*ψυχή*) is the total personality, with a 'spirit' (*πνεῦμα*) belonging to it: see especially Enoch xvi 1, and *J T S* viii 445.

[4] assigned] *ἐκρίθησαν* G = Aram. אתחתך or Heb. נחתך: see Dan ix 24 LXX.

[5] *ἐποίησαν* G, also E. Charles emends to *ἐποιήθησαν*, and this no doubt gives the required sense, but possibly the preceding words are a *nominativus pendens*, and *ἐποίησαν* may be the 3rd pers. plur. taken impersonally, as so often in Aramaic, also Lk xii 20 (*αἰτοῦσιν*).

appointed time and season, when the great judgement shall be upon
them.'

5 I noticed [the spirit][1] of a dead man petitioning, and its voice
even to heaven was going forth and petitioning, 6 and I asked Raphael,
the angel that was with me and said to him 'This spirit petitioning,
whose is it, that its voice so goes forth and petitions even unto
heaven?' 7 And he answered me, saying 'This spirit is what came
out from Abel, whom Cain his brother slew, and Abel is petitioning
about him, until his seed be destroyed from off the earth, and from
the seed of men his seed shall vanish'.

8 Then I asked about all the hollows, why they were separated one
from the other? 9 And he answered me, saying 'These three were
made that the spirits of the dead should be separated, and this one [2]
was separated for the spirits of the just, where the fountain of water
is shining. 10 And this one (of the three)[2] was created [for the
spirits] of the sinners when they die and are buried in the earth, and
no judgement has befallen them in their life. 11 Here their spirits are
separated for this great torment until the great day of the judgement,
of the scourgings, and of the torments of the accursed for ever; the
requital[3] of the spirits shall bind them there for ever. 12 And this
one[2] was separated for the spirits of those that are petitioning, who
make disclosures about their destruction when they have been slain
in the days of the sinners. 13 And this[2] was created for the spirits of
the men who will not be pious nor ungodly sinners,[4] and yet with the
lawless will be partakers; but these spirits, because those who suffer
here are less punished than the others, will not be sentenced in the
day of judgement, nor will they be raised from thence.'

14 Then I blessed the Lord of Glory, and said 'Blessed be Thou,
O Lord of righteousness, who art Lord of eternity!'

In *v.* 5 G has *τεθέαμαι ἀνθρώπουσ νεκροὺσ ἐντυγχάνοντοσ* (*sic*), E has 'I saw the spirits of men who were dead and their voice went forth. . . .' Lods and Charles, seeing that in the next verse only one petitioning spirit is referred to, suggest that the original Greek was *τεθέαμαι πνεῦμα ἀνθρώπου νεκροῦ ἐντυχάνοντοσ*.

It may be further remarked that according to Enoch lxxxi 6 the whole book is supposed to be written in the year preceding Enoch's

[1] For the text, see below.

[2] this one (*οὗτοσ*)] *οὕτωσ* GE, in all four places.

[3] read *ἡ ἀνταπόδοσισ* for *ην. αντ.*

[4] See note below for the text.

translation. If we take the Masoretic chronology (as is suitable for a Palestinian book) this year is 986 A.M. But Enoch's journeys and visions fall before that time; in fact, xxxii 6 assumes that the aged Adam and Eve are still alive. This explains how it is that the hollow gorges are all empty, except for the πνεῦμα of Abel: at the time when Enoch saw them only Abel is dead of all the human race. Had the LXX chronology been followed, Enoch must have seen the πνεύματα of Adam and Seth, if not others. Thus a consideration of this chapter makes it clear that Enoch is Palestinian.

v. 13ª runs in G *και ουτωσ εκτισθη τοισ πνευμασιν των ανθρωπων οσοι ουκ εσονται οσιοι αλλ αμαρτωλοι, οσοι ασεβεισ, και μετα των ανομων εσονται μετοχοι.*

Variants of E *εσονται*] 'were' E *οσιοι* (=חסידי)] 'righteous' E *οσο ασεβεισ*] 'who are complete in transgression' E *ανομων*] 'transgressors' E

It is evident that E only represents the same text as G, and failed to make any sense of it. *ὅσοι ἀσεβεῖσ* reads like mere 'translation Greek', as if the original translator was uncertain of the meaning. But the general sense of the whole passage, together with the clear words *οὐκ . . . ὅσιοι* and (in 13ᵇ) *οὐ τιμωρηθήσονται ἐν ἡμέρᾳ τῆσ κρίσεωσ*, makes it evident that these 'spirits' are some intermediate class between the pious and the wicked. I venture to suggest that the original to which *οὐκ—ἀλλ'* corresponds was not לא—אלא but לא—ולא, i.e. *neither—nor*. The Greek of Enoch according to this ought to have run *ὅσοι οὐκ ἔσονται ὅσιοι οὐδὲ ἁμαρτωλοὶ ἀσεβεῖσ*, the following *καί* having the Semitic sense of 'but'. *ἁμαρτωλοὶ ἀσεβεῖσ* is a combination assured for the Greek Enoch by i 9, but I do not know exactly what Semitic formula is intended.

With regard to the general picture sketched in Enoch xxii the most noticeable thing is the separate place assigned to the 'spirits' of the slain, especially when unburied. This is altogether in accordance with ancient, as distinct from modern thought. With us moderns the seemly disposal of dead bodies is mainly a matter of sentiment and hygiene; with the ancients, on the other hand, spilt blood and corpses not properly interred with due rites remained both a source of discomfort to the dead and an active pollution to the land in which they lay. Of the righteous, speaking generally, it was believed that 'their bodies are buried in peace';[1] but in Abel's case, though he may have been 'righteous', his spirit cannot rest with the righteous because he has been slain. In the Christian Apocalypse of John the 'souls' of those slain for the word of God, though they are kept underneath the heavenly Altar, yet cannot rest.

[1] Cf. also Isaiah liii 9.

4. *Miscellaneous Conjectures and Notes to Enoch.*

Enoch x 4 Δῆσον τὸν ’Αζαὴλ ποσὶν καὶ χερσίν, καὶ βάλε αὐτὸν εἰσ τὸ σκότοσ. These words are so like Matt xxii 13, that it is not unreasonable to suggest that they may have been the actual model for the form of words in the Gospel. If this be granted, it almost inevitably decides the text of Matt xxii 13 in favour of that attested by ℵB and Westcott and Hort against that of D latt and v. Soden, in which latter there is no mention of ‘binding’ (see *Evangelion da-Mepharreshe* ii 170).

Enoch x 7 that all the sons of men may not perish ἐν τῷ μυστηρίῳ ὅλῳ ᾧ ἐπάταξαν οἱ ἐγρήγοροι. This is nonsense, though G and E agree word for word. The Syncellus by substituting εἶπον for ἐπάταξαν tries to make a sort of sense, but it is most improbable that if ‘said’ was the original it should have been corrupted in any language into ‘smitten’. I venture to suggest that the text of G is correct, and that ἐν τῷ μυστηρίῳ stands for ברז in the Syriac sense of ‘after the manner of’ (e. g. *Carm. Nis.* xxix 22). The original Aramaic of this sentence, then, will be

ברז כל דמחו עיריא וחוו לבניהון

and the meaning of the whole passage will be

> ‘that the sons of men may not perish after the manner of all those whom the Watchers smote, when they taught their sons (the unlawful arts) and all the earth was made a desert with the works of Azael’s teaching’.

The ‘and’ before ἔδειξαν, here translated ‘when’, carries on the construction as in Apoc i 1 καὶ ἐσήμανεν, and Apoc vii 14 καὶ ἔπλυναν.

Enoch xii 4 τὸ ἁγίασμα τῆσ στάσεωσ τοῦ αἰῶνοσ. Charles translates this ‘the holy eternal place’ in apposition to ‘the high heaven’. But στάσισ can hardly be a ‘place’, except in the sense of ‘an appointed place’ for some one to stand in. The context says that the Watchers left high heaven, τὸ ἁγίασμα τῆσ στάσεωσ τοῦ αἰῶνοσ. Put back into Aramaic all is clear. στάσισ is קיים, i. e. covenant, as in the Targums to Gen ix 16: the Watchers left the sanctuary of the eternal covenant, and were defiled with women. The Watchers were like the *Bnai Ḳyāmā* in the early Syriac-speaking Church, and they left their *Ḳyāmā*, their ‘status’, as Professor Wensinck would translate it. But their ‘status’, as also always with the *Bnai Ḳyāmā*, implied abstinence from marriage.

Enoch xiv 11, 12 And its roof (αἱ στέγαι, of the House of God in heaven) was like the path of the stars and lightnings . . . . and οὐρανὸσ αὐτῶν ὕδωρ [12] καὶ πῦρ φλεγόμενον κύκλῳ τῶν τοίχων. The mention of 'water' comes in very oddly here : possibly the Aramaic corresponding to ὕδωρ καὶ may have been דמיין ל, i.e. 'like to', דמיין being plural to agree with שמיהון. The passage would then mean 'the ceiling thereof was like to flaming fire round about the walls'.

Enoch xx (The List of the Great Angels). It would add a little to the order and form of 'Enoch' to treat this chapter as a sort of Note or Heading, like Isaiah xxx 6[a]. It merely serves to introduce the names and functions of the several Angels mentioned in the course of Enoch's journeys.

Enoch xxvii 2 in the day of judgement . . . . here shall the ungodly (οἱ ἀσεβεῖσ) bless the Lord of Glory. For ἀσεβεῖσ E reads 'merciful' or 'gentle',—a mere guess. Dr Charles also does not accept ἀσεβεῖσ, and emends it into εὐσεβεῖσ. But the following verse shews that the ungodly are intended: 'in the days of their judgement they shall bless Him, in mercy, as He has allotted to them', i.e. the ungodly will as a favour be allowed to bless God. Compare Enoch lxiii, in which the mighty and the kings in their punishment say 'We have now learnt that we should glorify and bless the Lord of kings'.

Possibly in the original ἐν ἐλέει stood for something meaning a cry *for* mercy.

Enoch xxix 2 ἴδον κρίσεωσ δένδρα. Charles, following Beer and Praetorius, emends 'trees of judgement (דדינא)' into 'trees of smell (דריחא)'. But this does not account for the abnormal order. Read, therefore, בדין ('there') instead of דדין, so that the clause runs 'I saw there trees blowing spices'.

Enoch lxix 9, 10. It is perhaps worth notice that what is here blamed is not writing in itself, but written contracts. What the evil Pēnēmūe taught mankind was the Art of legal documents, secured with curses, &c., or binding formulae, whereby a man's mere word became of no account: cf. Matt v 37. Books in themselves, especially the 'Books of Enoch' (cf. civ 12), are good and a joy to the righteous.

Enoch cii 2, 3. Dr Charles regards the beginning of cii 3 as corrupt and says 'I cannot emend'. But is anything more needed than to transfer the first line of cii 3 to the preceding verse? The passage then runs

'2 And all the luminaries shall be affrighted with great fear, and all the earth shall be affrighted and tremble and be alarmed, and all the [holy] angels shall execute their commands.

'3 And [men] shall seek to hide themselves from the Great Glory, and the children of earth shall tremble and quake; And ye sinners shall be cursed for ever'.

5. *On the Astronomical teaching of Enoch.*

As remarked on p. 21 the Third Book of Enoch (lxxii–lxxxii) is almost wholly astronomical. It teaches that the heavenly bodies complete the year in 364 days (lxxiv 12), according to Enoch, and great stress is laid upon the perfection of this arrangement, whereby the year is exactly 52 weeks long. This has seemed a difficulty, for two reasons. On the one hand we have to explain why the author or editor of our Enoch thought it appropriate to insert a scientific treatise in his work, In chapters lxxii–lxxix, to quote Dr. Charles, "the author's interest is scientific," and "through all these chapters there is not a single ethical reference' (*Introd.*, p. 169). "But," he goes on to say, "in lxxx 2–8 the interest is ethical and nothing else, and though it recognizes an order of nature, this order is more conspicuous in its breach than in its observance." On the other hand it is a little disconcerting to find a writer like the author of lxxii–lxxix, who is so much interested in the Sun and Moon and the exact times and manner of their rising and setting, who yet can assert that the astronomical year is only 364 days long. And this as late as the 1st century B.C.!

It seems to me that a fresh view is possible and that our author was really a better practical astronomer than his modern critics imagine. I think he was quite aware that in the wicked days of the Seleucids the solstices and midsummer only came round after 365 or even 366 days.

This I take to be the meaning of chapter lxxx. In the days of the sinners, says Enoch, many bad things will happen. Amongst others 'the moon shall alter her orbit and not appear in her time,

. . . . and many chiefs of the stars shall transgress the order, and these shall alter their orbits and tasks and not appear at the seasons prescribed to them' (*vv.* 4, 5). It is true that Enoch lxxx 2 says that 'the years shall be shortened', but what this means is clear from *ver.* 3, where it says that 'the fruits of the earth shall be backward and will not grow in their time'. This happens, of course, when the official Kalendar Year is too short: what Enoch had observed was that according to the reckoning of 364 days in the year, which he believed to have been divinely ordained, the harvest would come too late. The times were, literally, out of joint owing to the misconduct of men and angels. This being the case, we see why Raguel takes vengeance upon the luminaries (ἐκδικῶν, both in xx 4 and xxiii 4). The Laws of Heaven are indeed inflexible, but Sun and Moon have a certain degree of freedom, which they, like men, have misused. This also was the teaching of Bardaisan (*De Fato*, § 10: see *Early Eastern Christianity*, p. 168). The interest of lxxii–lxxviii is therefore not purely scientific, but is ethical, like the rest of the whole work. It describes the *ideal* arrangement of the heavenly bodies, but Enoch indicates that they, like men, are transgressors and must come to judgement.

APPENDIX II.

ON THE MARTYRDOM OF ISAIAH.

THE pseudo-historical introduction to the Visions in the *Ascension of Isaiah*, commonly supposed to be a Jewish Legend, has been treated in the body of this work as a Greek Christian romance, especially composed so as to put the Visions in a historical setting.[1] In itself this theory needs less defence than one which should regard the fantastic tale as Jewish and of independent origin, and I shall not attempt a formal demonstration. The object of this Note is mainly explanatory, to point out one or two expressions in the story which seem to me to spring from dependence upon the Greek Bible rather than from Semitic lore.

The *Ascension of Isaiah* is preserved in a very ancient MS of the original Greek (G), in a very ancient Latin translation (L), and in an Ethiopic version (E). A different Latin version and a Slavonic version of the latter part of the work do not call here for special mention.

It should be remembered that the text of the Books of Kings (3 and 4 Regn), as they stand in the great uncials A and B, are a late revision greatly influenced by Origen. Where extant, the Old Latin gives an earlier type of text than either A or B or the so-called 'Lucian'.

Asc. Is. ii 5 'Sadduc' is the reading of G, changed by the editors into 'Zadok', who remark "The spelling ϹΑΔΔΟΥΚ is not found in the LXX, where the normal form is Σαδώκ" (*Amherst Papyri*, p. 17). But in Ezekiel the Greek Bible has Σαδδούκ, and in the Historical Books this form is usual in Lucian, including 4 Regn xv 33, where the Latins have 'Saddoc' (*Vind.*) and 'Sadduc' (*Lucca*). And in the genealogy of Ezra, both according to the Greek of 1 Ezra viii 2 and 2 Ezra vii 2, the name of Solomon's high Priest is Σάδδουκοσ or Σαδδούκ, not Σαδώκ. It looks very much as if in New Testament times there was no difference between 'Zadokites' and 'Sadducees': possibly צָדוֹק (*Zadok*, *Ṣādōḳ*) is a later and artificial form.[2]

[1] See above, p. 45 ff.

[2] The oldest testimony to 'Zadok' is Josephus's Σάδωκοσ. Josephus was a Pharisee.

Asc. Is. ii 9 ΙCΑCΟΥΦ (also ΙΑCΟΥΒ, iv 1), the son of Isaiah. This is, of course, the person called in Isai vii 3 Shear-jashub, but the LXX speaks of him as ὁ καταλειφθεὶσ Ἰασούβ. The Targum, on the other hand, has 'a remainder that have not sinned and that have repented from sin, thy disciple' (*sic*). In picking out the last two syllables of Shear-jashub as alone representing a personal name, the *Ascension* thus goes with the Greek Bible against Jewish lore.

Asc. Is. ii 12 the 400 prophets τῆσ Βάαλ. In treating Baal as feminine the *Ascension* follows a method which no doubt was originally Jewish (בעל = בשת), but which now only survives in Greek, e.g. Soph i 4; 4 Regn i 2 A, 6 AB, 16 AB; xxi 3. In a great many places in our present text of the Greek Bible 'Baal' has become masculine again (as of course it ought to be), probably through the influence of Origen; but that this is not original is suggested by S. Paul's quotation of 3 Regn xix 18 which has τῇ Βάαλ, while A and B have τῷ Βάαλ.

Asc. Is. ii 16 Ὀχοζείαν βασίλεα Γομόρρων. By the context, this is Ahaziah, king of Samaria. "Probably שמרון was misread עמרה," says Dr Charles! But the genitive of 'Gomorrha' in Greek is Γομόρρασ (e.g. *Asc.* iii 10). More probably therefore ΓΟΜΟΡΡΩΝ is a miswriting of ΣΟΜΟΡΩΝ, the alternative Greek name for Samaria (Isai vii 9, also 3 Regn xvi 24 Lucian, and 2 Ezra xiv 2).

Asc. Is. iii 2 ὄρη Μήδων. Thither was Israel carried captive, according to 4 Regn xvii 6, xviii 11, in the Greek: the Masoretic text has 'cities', not 'mountains'.

Asc. Is. iii 5 τῶν παίδων Ἐζεκίου. The Greek of the Historical Books tends to distinguish (in the plural) between the δοῦλοι who are bondmen or else worshippers of a God, and the παῖδεσ who are officials of a king, both classes being represented by the same Hebrew. The παῖδεσ of King Hezekiah, for instance, are mentioned in 4 Regn xix 5, so that here also the *Ascension of Isaiah* conforms to the phraseology of the Greek Bible.

Asc. Is. iii 6. Isaiah is accused of prophesying that Jerusalem and Judah shall go into captivity ἐν γαλεάγρᾳ (*sic*) καὶ ἐν πέδαισ (iii 6). This word γαλεάγρα is from the nature of the case not of very common occurrence, as it seems to mean a sort of trap. But it comes in Ezek xix 9, where Jehoiachin being taken captive to Babylon is compared to a lion brought home alive in a trap or cage. Here again the choice of words in the *Ascension* is derived from the Greek Bible.

Asc. Is. iii 15 τοῦ ἀγγέλου τῆσ 'Εκκλησίασ τῆσ ἐν οὐρανῷ. Here the Ethiopic is said to have "the angel of the Christian Church which is in the heavens". It may be worth while to point out that this gross contravention of the rule not prematurely to name names in prophecy is only the result of awkward translation. The regular rendering of ἐκκλησία in Ethiopic (e.g. Acts viii 1) is "House of Christians"; here the Ethiopic has "the angel of the House-of-Christians", but this simply corresponds word for word to τοῦ ἀγγέλου τῆσ 'Εκκλησίασ.

Asc. Is. ii 4 'Beliar whose name is *Maṭanbūchūs*', v 3 'in *Mĕchēmbēchus*'.[1] So the Ethiopic: most unfortunately neither the Greek nor the Latin is extant at either place. In the *Ascension of Isaiah* Beliar is "the angel of lawlessness, the ruler of this world", the great opponent of the Christ and the true doctrine about the Christ. But he does not appear in a separate visible form. He sits *upon* Manasse (i 9),[2] *in the heart of* Manasse and his princes (iii 11, v 1). The story of the actual Martyrdom runs thus: Beliar was wrath with Isaiah and sat in the heart of Manasse, [2] and while Isaiah was being sawn asunder Balchira (the false prophet) stood accusing him, [3] and Balchira by [*or*, in] Mĕchēmbēchūs stood (pl.) mocking, [4] and Beliar said to Isaiah 'Say, the ways of Balchira are good . . . [8] and I will turn the heart of Manasse'. . . . . [15] These things did Beliar to Isaiah by the hand of Balchira and by the hand of Manasse.[3]

It is clear from this that Beliar is speaking out of the mouth of Balchira. But just before he was 'in the heart of Manasse'. Beliar therefore goes from one to the other. Is not this *metempsychosis*? It seems to me that *ba-mĕchēmbēchūs* in v 3 stands for διὰ μετεμψυχώσεωσ and that in ii 4 *Maṭanbūchūs* stands for μετέμψυχοσ, or some such form.

[1] See above, p. 46, note. [2] i. e. M. is 'devil-ridden', as in the Syriac phrase.
[3] v 1-15, compressed.

APPENDIX III.

ON SOME OTHER KINDS OF APOCALYPSES.

In the three Schweich Lectures it was impossible to pass in review all Jewish and Christian Apocalypses. In the first place I have said very little directly about the New Testament, because I considered that the matter in itself is familiar, and its discussion, to be profitable, would need extended treatment. Mk xiii, or 1 Cor xv, alone would require a whole Lecture. But besides the New Testament there are other well-known works which I have passed over. This has not been from considerations of space, but because I venture to think they belong to an essentially different order of thought and represent a different movement from that which produced the Jewish Apocalypses and gave birth to the Christian Church. Two of these call for special mention.

The *Book of the Secrets of Enoch* (called also 2 Enoch), preserved only in Slavonic and edited by Dr Charles in 1896, is a work composed in Greek, apparently in Egypt. It teaches that there are seven heavens, that the year is 365¼ days long (i. e. the Julian reckoning), and that this world will last 7000 years. There is nothing about a Messiah, Christian or Jewish. It is evident that, even if we allow for a millennial reign on earth at the end of this state of things, the author does not expect it to begin for some 800 years. In other words, the practical outlook of the Slavonic Enoch upon the world is utterly different from that of the Jewish Apocalypses considered in this volume and from that of the New Testament. In these the End of all things is at hand, in the Slavonic Enoch the world is comparatively stable and the End is far off.

When we ask what the date of the Slavonic Enoch is, or what kind of person compiled it, no very certain answer can be given. Dr Charles (*Introd.* § 5) has collected together a number of parallels with early Christian literature, comprising e. g. the passages which assume the existence of seven heavens, or the derivation of the name *Adam* from the initial letters of the four quarters of the world Ἀνατολή, Δύσισ, Ἄρκτοσ, Μεσημβρία. But in no instance is the literary connexion assured. It appears to me that this is one of the many cases in which we ought to take account of the choice of pseudonym. The only passage which has been held to prove a date before 70 A. D. is lix 2, in which the offering of clean beasts as a sacrifice is mentioned, and 'sacrifices could only be offered in Jerusalem' (Charles, on 2 Enoch li 4). But the whole book is supposed to be written before the Flood, long before the promulgation of the Mosaic Law. Enoch's 'sons' are all mankind, and the book actually closes with an account of Methusalem's sacrifice to the Lord on the occasion of his father Enoch's translation (lxviii 5, 6). I do not know that a Christian romance of Enoch need differ very much from a Jewish romance of Enoch. And further, the whole question of the channels by which rare and curious literature found their way into Slavonic requires fresh and independent investigation.[1]

The Apocalypses of *Elias* and *Sophonias* and the other works edited by Steindorff in *T. u. U.* (N.F.) ii *3a* in 1899 are most curious documents. The MSS from which they are edited are very ancient (4th or 5th cent.), though unfortunately they are mere fragments, like most early Coptic MSS. For our present purpose, the special interest of the *Apocalypse of Elias* is that it is generally supposed to be Jewish, or at least that its subject-matter is derived directly from Jewish legends. I have come to doubt this, and to think that the Jewish colouring of parts of the book is to be explained by the same rule as I have used to explain the universalism of Enoch, *viz.* that if a work professes to be the work of a Jewish Prophet it was not considered appropriate that it should be too explicitly Christian, especially in the naming of names. It may be noticed here that the story of Susanna is mentioned (p. 151), and the name Shadrach appears in the form *Searak*[2] (*ibid.*). Further, the true Messiah will be distinguished by the sign of the Cross (p. 161), while Antichrist, for all his miraculous powers, will be unable to raise the dead or have power over life (ψυχή). I cannot help thinking that S. Cyril of Jerusalem knew of this book, or something very like it, and that it forms the background of the picture of Antichrist at Jerusalem, given by Cyril in *Catechesis* xv 14, 15, notwithstanding his express profession of relying on no 'apocryphal' document.

[1] I wonder that in the new edition of 2 Enoch (*Apocrypha and Pseudepigrapha* ii p. 437) no notice is taken of M. R. James's discovery that in xv 1 'every bird' should be 'every cock', and that what the cock says at cockcrow is given in xv 2[a]: see *Apocrypha Anecdota II*, p. lxv.

[2] i. e. ⲥⲉⲁⲣⲁⲕ for ⲥⲉⲇⲣⲁⲕ (or ⲥⲉⲇⲣⲁⲭ).

Further investigation may possibly reveal a genuine Jewish element in these Egyptian works, but it seems to me that they owe a great deal more to native ideas of appropriate punishment meted out to individual evildoers as they arrive after death in Hell. Coptic writers freely borrow their vocabulary from Greek, but they always use the vernacular for *Amente*, where all the souls of the dead are collected from the Flood to the present day (p. 152).

والله اعلم

INDEX

GENESIS — PAGE
- ix 16 (Targ.) 68
- xv 18 12 n.
- xl 23 (Targ.) 55

LEVITICUS
- xvi 10 28
- xxii 14 65

DEUTERONOMY
- iii 9 28

2 SAMUEL
- xx 18 30

1 (3) KINGS
- xvi 24, xix 18 73

2 (4) KINGS
- i 2, 6, 16 73
- xv 33 72
- xvii 6, xviii 11 73
- xix 5 73

EZRA (*see below*)

JOB
- Author of 19

PSALMS
- xix (xviii) 13, 14 (Aq) 65

CANTICLES
- iv 8 28

ISAIAH
- vii 3, 9 (Lxx) 73
- xxx 6[a] 69

EZEKIEL
- xix 9 (Lxx) 73
- xxix 15 7 n.

DANIEL
- Book of 6, 11, 23, 33, 42, 45, 46
- iv 17 7
- vii 9 23
- vii 19 41
- ix 24 (Lxx) 65 n.
- xi 30 19 n.

S. MATTHEW
- v 37 69
- xii 7 8
- xii 26–30 22
- xii 43–45 21 f.
- xxii 13 68
- xxv 31–46 23–25

S. MARK
- ix 20 22 n.
- xiii 40, 44, 49

S. LUKE
- xi 18–23 22
- xi 24–28 21 f.
- xii 20 65 n.

ROMANS — PAGE
- xi 4 73

1 CORINTHIANS
- xv 24 ff. 43 n.
- xv 46 25
- xv 51 43 n.

2 CORINTHIANS
- vi 15 45 n.

2 TIMOTHY
- iii 16 10

1 PETER
- iii 19 10

JUDE
- 9 39
- 13–15 10, 17

REVELATION
- i 1 68
- i 9–11 6
- vi 9–11 48, 67
- vi 15 37 n.
- vii 9–17 48
- vii 14 68
- xiv 13 48
- xvi 7 48 n.

---

1 EZRA (= *First Esdras*)
- viii 2 72

2 EZRA (= *Ezra-Nehemiah*)
- vii 2 72
- xiv 2 73

4 EZRA (= *Second Esdras*)
- Author of 19, 41 f.
- vii 26–44 42 n., 43 n.
- vii 50 32
- vii 64 f., 116 43
- ix 22 43
- xi f. 41

1 MACCABEES
- v 23, 45 ff. 35

2 MACCABEES
- vi, vii 16, 39 n.

BARUCH (*Apocalypse of*)
- Not composite 41
- lxxii 4–6 25
- lxxvii 6, 16 42
- lxxxv 3 8, 15, 42

ENOCH (*Book of*) — PAGE
- Author and tendency 10 f., 17 ff., 28 ff.
- Contents 20
- MSS and Versions :—
  - Cairo (Gizeh) MS 26 f., 53 f., 62 f., 68
  - Ethiopic Version 26, 54, 55 n., 62 f., 68
  - Syncellus Quotations 26, 53 f., 68
  - Vatican Fragment 26
- Originally in Aramaic or Hebrew 27, 68, 69
- Uses Heb. text (not Lxx) 67

(*In the following list * distinguishes passages explained or emended.*)

- i–v 56–61
- *i 2 64
- *i 5 64
- *i 7 63
- i 9 17, 67
- *ii 2 65
- *ii 3–v 1 63
- *v 6 63 f.
- *v 8 65
- vi 1–6 53 ff.
- *vi 6 54 f.
- vii 1 (Sync.) 27
- vii 2 (Sync.) 55
- viii 4 27
- x 4 28, 68
- *x 7 68
- x 17 27
- *xii 14 68
- *xiii 7, 9 28 f.
- *xiv 11, 12 69
- xv, xvi 22
- xv 11 55
- xvi 1 27, 65
- *xviii 13 ff., xxi 6 31 n.
- xx 69
- xxii 1–14 65 f.
- *xxii 13 20 n., 67
- *xxiii 4 71
- xxvi f. 28
- *xxvii 2 69
- *xxix 2 69
- xxxii 6 67
- xxxviii 5 37 n.
- xlvi 23
- lxii–lxiii 10 23 f., 49
- *lxii 6 37 n., 49

PAGE
lxix 9, 10 69
lxxii–lxxxii 21, 70 f.
*lxxiv 12, lxxx 2 70
lxxxi 6 66
lxxxiii 1, lxxxv 2 18 n.
xciv–civ. 62
c 4 64
*cii 2, 3 70
civ 1, 2, 6. 32
civ 12 69
cv 2, cvi–cviii 55 n.

ISAIAH
(*Ascension of*)
Tendency of 45 ff.
i 9 74
ii 4 74
ii 5 72
ii 9 73
ii 12 73
ii 16 73
iii 2 73
iii 5 73
iii 6 73
iii 13 ff. 47
iii 15 74
iv 2 46
v 1 47, 74
v 3 74
v 14 45
xi 2–22 46

JUBILEES
iv 15 54
vii 22 55
xxvii 16 57 n.

MOSES
(*Assumption of*)
19, 37–40

SOLOMON
(*Psalms of*)
xvii 37

XII PATRIARCHS
Reu vi 10 34
Jos xix 1 ff. 36 n.
Tendency of
15, 34 f., 47

Abel Beth-Ma'acha 30
Aboth, Pirkē 8 n., 9
A. D. 70, Effects of
4, 8 ff., 13, 40 ff., 76
Akiba 9, 12 n., 21
Amente 77
Antiochus Epiphanes
6, 33, 36, 42, 50
Apamea 30
Aquila 65
Asmoneans, *see* Maccabees
Azael (Azazel) 20, 28, 68

PAGE
Baal (fem.) 73
Bacher, W. 8 n.
Bardaisan 71
Barnabas, Ep. of 10
Beliar 45 f., 74
Bereshith rabba 44 12 n.
Bevan, Edwyn 7, 30 f.
Box, G. H. 42

Canon, Jewish 9, 11, 15
Charles, R. H. 26 f., 34,
35 n., 37 n., 54, 63,
65 f., 69 f., 73, 75
Civilization,
4, 6, 20, 32, 49
Cosmos, the 7, 21, 31 f.
Cyril (of Jerus.) 76

Dan, Waters of 28
Dante 2, 44 f.
Demons 22 f., 31
Didache 44
Doublets (in Enoch) 63

Eliou(d) 55
Enoch (Slavonic) 75 f.
Ephraim Syrus
Carm. Nis. xxix 22 68
Esdras, *see* 4 Ezra
Ev. da-Mepharreshē 68

Galilee 30, 35
Geoponica xi 1 63
Gospels, Synoptic
21 ff., 40

Hadrian 8, 42
Hadudo, Beth 28
Hermon 28 f., 54
Herod 11, 37 f.
Hort 62, 68
Hyrcanus, John 30, 35 f.

Incarnation, the 47
Inconsistencies 48 f.

James, M. R. 39 n., 76 n.
Jamnia 8 n., 11
Jannaeus 11
Jared 53 ff.
Jerome, *De V. Ill.* 17
Johanan b. Zakkai
8 n., 10, 12, 15, 42
Jordan, Sources of 28 f.
Josephus 11, 35, 72 n.
Joshua b. Ḥanania 8 n.
Journ. of Theol. Studies
viii 445 65 n.
x 135 35
xiii 374 19

PAGE
Judaism and Hellen-
ism 4, 6, 8, 25, 30 f., 50
Judgement, Last 2f., 13,
23 ff., 31 f., 43, 49, 71

Kingdom of God
7, 12 f., 15, 22
Kipling 20 n.
Ḳyama, Bnai 68

Maccabees 16, 35, 37 f.
Martyrs, Maccabean
6 f., 36, 42
Mead, G. R. S. 18 n.
Messiah 37, 43
see also Son of Man
Metempsychosis 46 n., 74

Nephilim 27, 55
Nero redivivus 46

Peter, Apocalypse of 44
Philo 5
Pistis Sophia 354 18 n.
Posidonius 30 ff.
Pseudonymity 5 f., 19, 76

Qoran liv 1 39 n.

Rabbinic Religion
8, 14, 30
Reitzenstein 30 n.

Salathiel 41
Simon the Just 8 n.
Son of Man 20, 23 f.
Sophonias, Ap. of 76
Sources, lost,
reconstruction of 41, 62
Spirit 22, 65 n.
Stars 3, 30 f., 70 f.
Stoics 3, 30 f.,
Syncellus, *see* Enoch
Syncretism 3, 30

Taxo (Eleazar) 39 n., 40
Tertullian 10, 18, 39

Vergil, *Geor.* ii 490 32
Visions 40 f.

Wellhausen 9
Wensinck, A. J. 68

Year, length of 70 f., 75

Zadok, Ṣaddūḳ 72